HEALTHY
fAMILY fOOD
a new approach

A J.B. Fairfax Press Publication

INTRODUCTION

This book takes a look at the way we can all improve our diets by including more vegetables. While it is not a vegetarian book, many of the recipes will appeal to vegetarians.

A well-balanced diet can be guided by three rules: eat most of vegetables, fruit, breads and cereals; eat moderately of lean meat, chicken, fish, seafood, eggs and dairy products; eat least of fats, sugar and salt. It is well known that many people eat most of the foods which should be present only in small quantities. They also neglect the foods which should dominate the diet – especially vegetables.

This book reminds us of the great variety of vegetables available and has a wealth of wonderful recipes which will give vegetables their rightful place as hero of the meal.

EDITORIAL
Food Editor: Rachel Blackmore
Editors: Margaret Gore, Kirsten John, Linda Venturoni
Editorial and Production Assistant: Danielle Thiris
Editorial Coordinator: Margaret Kelly
UK Food Consultant: Katie Swallow

Photograhy: Quentin Bacon
Food and Styling: Susan Dodd
Assistant Recipe Development: Penny Farrell
Assistant Food Stylist: Michelle Gorry
Cover Stylist: Donna Hay

DESIGN AND PRODUCTION
Manager: Sheridan Carter
Layout and Design: Lulu Dougherty
Senior Production Editor: Anna Maguire
Production Editor: Sheridan Packer
Cover Design: Michele Withers

Published by J.B. Fairfax Press Pty Limited
80-82 McLachlan Ave
Rushcutters Bay, NSW, 2011 Australia
A.C.N. 003 738 430

Formatted by J.B. Fairfax Press Pty Limited
Printed by Toppan Printing Co., Singapore
PRINTED IN SINGAPORE

The Custom Book Company is a joint venture of Century Magazines Pty Limited A.C.N. 003 400 904 and R.A. Ramsey Pty Limited A.C.N. 001 864 446

JBFP 373
Includes Index
1 86343 208 6

DISTRIBUTION AND SALES
United Kingdom: J.B. Fairfax Press Limited
Ph: (0933) 40 2330 Fax: (0933) 40 2234

ABOUT THIS BOOK

INGREDIENTS

Unless otherwise stated the following ingredients are used in this book:

Cream	Double, suitable for whipping
Flour	White flour, plain or standard
Sugar	White sugar

WHAT'S IN A TABLESPOON?

AUSTRALIA
1 tablespoon = 20 mL or 4 teaspoons
NEW ZEALAND
1 tablespoon = 15 mL or 3 teaspoons
UNITED KINGDOM
1 tablespoon = 15 mL or 3 teaspoons
The recipes in this book were tested in Australia where a 20 mL tablespoon is standard. The tablespoon in the New Zealand and the United Kingdom sets of measuring spoons is 15 mL. For recipes using baking powder, gelatine, bicarbonate of soda, small quantities of flour and cornflour, simply add another teaspoon for each tablespoon specified.

CANNED FOODS

Can sizes vary between countries and manufacturers. You may find the quantities in this book are slightly different to what is available. Purchase and use the can size nearest to the suggested size in the recipe.

MICROWAVE IT

Where microwave instructions occur in this book, a microwave oven with a 650 watt output has been used. Wattage on domestic microwave ovens varies between 500 and 700 watts, so it may be necessary to vary cooking times slightly depending on the wattage of your oven.

CONTENTS

CABBAGE FAMILY

Brussels sprouts, broccoli, cauliflower and Chinese cabbage are 'kissing cousins', descendants of true cabbage, and share common characteristics which include a delicious sweetness when harvested after the first frost – and an unmistakably strong aroma if cooked too long! To bring out this family's best behaviour, keep the cooking to a minimum with these simply delicious ideas.

BRUSSELS SPROUTS IN PLUM SAUCE

2 tablespoons vegetable oil
500 g/1 lb Brussels sprouts, halved
1 red pepper, cut into thin strips
1 clove garlic, crushed
100 g/3^1/$_2$ oz snow peas (mangetout)
100 g/3^1/$_2$ oz button mushrooms, halved
3 spring onions, chopped
1 tablespoon chopped fresh coriander or parsley
1 tablespoon plum sauce

1 Heat oil in a large frying pan or wok over a medium heat, add Brussels sprouts, red pepper and garlic and stir-fry for 2 minutes or until sprouts turn a bright green.

2 Add snow peas (mangetout), mushrooms, spring onions, coriander or parsley and plum sauce to pan and stir-fry for 2-3 minutes longer or until vegetables are just tender. Serve immediately.

Serves 6

Choose Brussels sprouts that are firm and compact, bright in colour, fresh-looking and are no larger than a golf ball. The small, younger sprouts have a superior flavour. Trim stem ends, remove any yellow outer leaves and rinse. To ensure even cooking, cut a shallow cross in the base.

Brussels Sprouts in Plum Sauce

Brussels Sprouts Gratin

500 g/1 lb Brussels sprouts
1 cup/250 mL/8 fl oz chicken stock
15 g/^{1}/$_2$ oz butter
1 tablespoon flour
^{1}/4 cup/15 g/^{1}/$_2$ oz breadcrumbs, made
from stale bread
1 tablespoon grated Parmesan cheese

1 Cut a cross in the base of each Brussels sprout. Place stock and Brussels sprouts in a saucepan, cover and bring to the boil over a medium heat. Reduce heat and simmer for 8 minutes or until sprouts are just tender. Drain sprouts and place a shallow ovenproof dish. Reserve stock.

2 Melt butter in a small saucepan over a medium heat, add flour and cook, stirring, for 1 minute. Remove pan from heat and gradually whisk in reserved stock. Return pan to heat and cook, stirring constantly, for 4-5 minutes until sauce boils and thickens.

3 Pour sauce over Brussels sprouts, sprinkle with breadcrumbs and Parmesan cheese and cook under a preheated hot grill for 3-4 minutes or until topping is golden.

Serves 4

The simplest presentations are often the best. Try steamed Brussels sprouts tossed in browned butter and sprinkled with chopped nuts or breadcrumbs.

Peperoni Cabbage

15 g/^{1}/$_2$ oz butter
1 tablespoon olive oil
125 g/4 oz peperoni, sliced
1 onion, chopped
1 red pepper, chopped
2 cloves garlic, crushed
250 g/8 oz cabbage, finely shredded

Heat butter and oil in a large frying pan or wok over a medium heat, add peperoni, onion, red pepper and garlic and stir-fry for 4 minutes, or until onion is soft. Add cabbage and stir-fry for 2-3 minutes longer or until vegetables are just tender. Serve immediately.

Serves 6

Buy cabbages that are solid and heavy for their size. Leaves should be crisp, compact and bright in colour. Avoid those with brown spots or yellow leaves. Store in the refrigerator in the crisper or place in a plastic food bag.

Chinese Cabbage Chow Mein

CHINESE CABBAGE CHOW MEIN

125 g/4 oz rice noodles
1 tablespoon vegetable oil
2 leeks, thinly sliced
125 g/4 oz ham, diced
2 teaspoons chopped fresh coriander
750 g/1$^1/_2$ lb Chinese cabbage, finely
shredded
$^1/_4$ cup/60 mL/2 fl oz teriyaki sauce
1 tablespoon oyster sauce

1   Place noodles in a bowl and pour
over enough cold water to cover. Soak
for 10-15 minutes or until tender.
Drain and set aside.

2   Heat oil in a large frying pan or wok
over a medium heat, add leeks, ham
and coriander and stir-fry for 1 minute
or until leeks are soft. Add cabbage and
stir-fry for 2 minutes or until vegetables
are just tender.

3   Add noodles, teriyaki sauce and
oyster sauce to vegetable mixture and
stir-fry for 3-4 minutes or until heated
through.

Serves 6

Chinese cabbage, also
known as Chinese leaves
resembles a pale head of
Cos lettuce with broad,
ribbed, pale-green, strongly
veined, wavy crinkled
leaves.

CAULIFLOWER BHAJI

45 g/1^1/$_2$ oz butter
1 tablespoon vegetable oil
1 teaspoon ground turmeric
1 teaspoon ground cumin
2 teaspoons finely chopped
fresh ginger
1 fresh red chilli, finely chopped
500 g/1 lb cauliflower, cut into florets
500 g/1 lb potatoes, cut into
2 cm/^{3}/$_4$ in cubes
^{1}/$_4$ cup/60 mL/2 fl oz water
^{1}/$_2$ cup/125 mL/4 fl oz chicken stock

1   Heat butter and oil in a frying pan over a medium heat, add turmeric, cumin, ginger and chilli and cook, stirring, for 1 minute or until fragrant. Add cauliflower, potatoes and water, cover and cook for 10 minutes or until vegetables are just tender.

2   Transfer vegetables to a serving dish, set aside and keep warm. Add stock to pan, bring to simmering and simmer until stock reduces by half. Pour stock over vegetables and serve immediately.

Serves 6

"Cauliflower is cabbage with a college education."
Mark Twain

CAULIFLOWER AND NUT SOUFFLES

Oven temperature
200°C, 400°F, Gas 6

45 g/1^1/$_2$ oz butter
250 g/8 oz cauliflower, cut into
small florets
2 tablespoons flour
1 cup/250 mL/8 fl oz milk
15 g/^{1}/$_2$ oz macadamia or Brazil nuts,
chopped and toasted
1 tablespoon French mustard
3 eggs, separated
2 egg whites

1   Melt butter in a saucepan over a medium heat, add cauliflower and flour and cook, stirring, for 1 minute. Remove pan from heat and gradually stir in milk. Return pan to heat and cook, stirring constantly, for 4-5 minutes or until mixture boils and thickens.

2   Remove pan from heat and set aside to cool slightly. Stir nuts, mustard and egg yolks into mixture.

3   Place the 5 egg whites in a clean bowl and beat until stiff peaks form. Fold egg whites into cauliflower mixture. Pour soufflé mixture into four 1 cup/250 mL/8 fl oz greased soufflé dishes and bake for 20 minutes or until soufflés are puffed and golden. Serve immediately.

Serves 4

Choose cauliflower that is firm, compact with creamy-white heads and florets pressed tightly together. A yellow tinge indicates a cauliflower past its best. Leaves should be bright green and crisp. Refrigerate unwashed, stored in a plastic food bag with head turned downwards.

Cauliflower Rarebit

CAULIFLOWER RAREBIT

1 cauliflower, trimmed
90 g/3 oz butter
$^1/_2$ cup/125 mL/4 fl oz cream (double)
or beer
2 teaspoons French mustard
2 teaspoons Worcestershire sauce
250 g/8 oz grated tasty cheese
(mature Cheddar)

1   Cut a cross in the base of the cauliflower stem. Boil, steam or microwave cauliflower until just tender. Place cauliflower in a shallow ovenproof dish and keep warm.

2   Melt butter in a saucepan over a medium heat, stir in cream or beer, mustard and Worcestershire sauce. Reduce heat to very low, add cheese and stir until cheese melts and sauce is smooth. Drizzle sauce over cauliflower and serve immediately.

Serves 6

This luscious cheesy sauce will taste just as marvellous over any other vegetables such as celery, zucchini (courgettes) or Brussels sprouts.

Autumn Vegetable Tempura

vegetable oil for deep-frying
250 g/8 oz broccoli, broken into
florets and thinly sliced
1 eggplant (aubergine), cut
crosswise into thin rounds

TEMPURA BATTER
1 cup/125 g/4 oz flour
1 cup/250 mL/8 fl oz iced water
1 egg yolk

OYSTER DIPPING SAUCE
$^1/_4$ cup/60 mL/2 fl oz soy sauce
1 tablespoon honey
2 teaspoons oyster sauce

HORSERADISH DIPPING SAUCE
$1^1/_2$ tablespoons olive oil
1 tablespoon horseradish cream
1 tablespoon water

1 To make batter, place flour, water and egg yolk into a bowl and whisk until smooth. Set aside to rest at room temperature for 30 minutes.

2 To make Oyster Dipping Sauce, place soy sauce, honey and oyster sauce in a small bowl, mix to combine and set aside. To make Horseradish Dipping Sauce, place olive oil, horseradish cream and water in a small bowl, mix to combine and set aside.

3 Heat vegetable oil in a large saucepan until a cube of bread browns in 50 seconds. Dip vegetables, a few pieces at a time, into batter and drain, allowing excess batter to run off. Cook in hot oil for 3-4 minutes or until tender and golden. Using a slotted spoon remove vegetables, drain on absorbent kitchen paper and serve immediately with dipping sauces.

Serves 6

Select fresh, bright-green broccoli which has compact clusters of tightly closed florets. Stalks and stem leaves should be tender yet firm. Avoid heads with yellowing florets and thick, woody stems. Keep dry. Store in a vented plastic food bag in refrigerator for up to 5 days.

Tasty Broccoli Muffins

Oven temperature
190°C, 375°F, Gas 5

Unusually different and delicious, these savoury muffins are wonderful with soup-and-salad meals.

2 cups/250 g/8 oz self-raising flour
$^1/_2$ teaspoon mixed spice
125 g/4 oz grated tasty cheese
(mature Cheddar)
375 g/12 oz broccoli, broken into
small florets
1 cup/250 mL/8 fl oz milk
1 egg, lightly beaten

1 Sift together flour and mixed spice into a bowl. Add cheese and broccoli and mix to combine. Stir in milk and egg, taking care not to overmix.

2 Spoon mixture into ten lightly greased 1 cup/250 mL/8 fl oz capacity muffin tins and bake for 30 minutes or until cooked when tested with a skewer. Serve hot, warm or cold.

Makes 10

Autumn Vegetable Tempura

'FRUIT' VEGETABLES

Because of their seeds, sweet peppers, eggplant (aubergines) and tomatoes are known as the 'fruits' of the vegetable kingdom. Because their flavours meld together so well, they've become the seasoning backbone of many a Mediterranean cook's repertoire. But don't overlook the fact that each of the trio has distinctive flavour and appeal when served on its own, as this selection of special recipes shows.

PEPPER AND SAUSAGE HOT POT

45 g/1¹/₂ oz butter
2 onions, chopped
3 cloves garlic, crushed
500 g/1 lb red peppers, quartered
500 g/1 lb green peppers, quartered
500 g/1 lb tomatoes, chopped
2 tablespoons chopped fresh oregano
or 1 teaspoon dried oregano
¹/₂ cup/125 mL/4 fl oz dry white wine
8 fresh spicy sausages
freshly ground black pepper

1 Melt butter in a frying pan over a medium heat, add onions and garlic and cook, stirring, for 5 minutes or until onions are golden.

2 Add red and green peppers, tomatoes, oregano and wine to pan and stir to combine. Bring to the boil, then reduce heat, cover and simmer for 20 minutes or until vegetables are tender.

3 Add sausages to pan, cover and simmer for 15-20 minutes longer or until sausages are cooked through. Season to taste with black pepper.

Serves 4

Sweet peppers are also called bell peppers because of their bell-like shape. If left on the stem to ripen, peppers change colour from bright green to red. Less common are the yellow, black or orange varieties.

Preserved Roasted Sweet Peppers

PRESERVED ROASTED SWEET PEPPERS

1 kg/2 lb mixed red, yellow and
green peppers
$^1/_2$ cup/125 mL/4 fl oz olive oil
$^1/_2$ cup/125 mL/4 fl oz white
wine vinegar
2 tablespoons sugar
3 sprigs fresh oregano or thyme
2 cloves garlic, peeled
1 fresh red chilli, chopped

1   Halve and seed peppers and place,
skin-side-up, under a preheated hot grill
and cook for 10 minutes or until skin
blisters and chars. Place in a plastic
food bag, seal and set aside until cool
enough to handle. Remove from bag,
peel off skin and discard. Cut peppers
into $^1/_2$-1 cm/$^1/_4$-$^1/_2$ in strips and place
in a sterilised jar.

2   Place oil, vinegar, sugar, oregano
or thyme, garlic and chilli in a
saucepan, bring to the boil over a
medium heat and cook, stirring
occasionally, until sugar dissolves. Pour
vinegar mixture over pepper strips in
jar, seal and allow to cool. Refrigerate
until required. Serve as antipasto, as an
accompaniment to meats or in salads.

Makes 3 cups/750 g/1$^1/_2$ lb

Select firm, well-shaped
peppers with glossy, smooth
skins. Avoid dull-looking
peppers with soft spots,
wrinkled skin or blemishes.
Store in the crisper section
of the refrigerator for up to
a week.

PORK AND MUSHROOM TIMBALES

Oven temperature
160°C, 325°F, Gas 3

500 g/1 lb thin eggplant (aubergines),
cut into 5 mm/^{1}/$_4$ in slices
salt
vegetable oil for shallow-frying
375 g/12 oz pork fillet, trimmed and
cut crosswise into 6 pieces

MUSHROOM FILLING
2 slices bread
125 g/4 oz button mushrooms,
roughly chopped
1 teaspoon chopped fresh rosemary or
^{1}/$_2$ teaspoon dried rosemary
freshly ground black pepper

3 To make filling, place bread, mushrooms, rosemary and black pepper to taste in a food processor or blender and process to make a smooth paste.

4 Line six 1 cup/250 mL/8 fl oz capacity timbale moulds or ramekins with eggplant (aubergine) slices by overlapping them evenly around the sides and over the base. Place a piece of pork in base of each timbale and top with any remaining eggplant (aubergine) slices. Cover with mushroom mixture, press down firmly.

Eggplant (aubergine) is usually 'degorged' before cooking by sprinkling the cut surfaces with salt and allowing to stand before rinsing thoroughly. This softens the eggplant (aubergine) and reduces the amount of oil it absorbs during cooking. Eggplant (aubergine) bruises easily so handle with care.

1 Place eggplant (aubergines) slices in a bowl set over a colander, sprinkle with salt and set aside to stand for 15-20 minutes. Rinse slices under cold running water, drain well and pat dry on absorbent kitchen paper.

2 Heat 1 cm/^{1}/$_2$ in oil in a frying pan over a medium heat and cook eggplant (aubergine) for 3-4 minutes each side or until golden. Drain and cool on absorbent kitchen paper.

5 Place timbales in a baking dish with enough boiling water to come halfway up the sides of the timbales. Cover dish with foil and bake for 20 minutes or until pork is cooked and tender. Turn onto serving plates.

Serves 6

GARLIC AND TAHINI DIP

Eggplant (aubergine) should be firm, heavy in relation to size, with a uniform dark purple colour or colour characteristic of the variety. Select those free of scars or cuts. Avoid dull, soft, shrivelled or blemished fruit. The sharper the prickles around the stalk the fresher the eggplant (aubergine). Store in refrigerator for up to a week.

1 kg/2 lb eggplant (aubergines),
halved lengthwise
2 cloves garlic, crushed
2 tablespoons chopped fresh parsley
2 tablespoons tahini (sesame seed
paste)
2 tablespoons lemon juice
pitta bread
selection raw vegetables such as carrot
and celery sticks, cauliflower and
broccoli florets and cherry tomatoes

Makes 1^1/$_2$ cups/375 g/12 oz

1 Place eggplant (aubergines), cut-side-down, under a preheated hot grill and cook for 15-20 minutes or until skin chars and blisters and pulp is soft. Set aside to cool.

2 Scoop pulp out of skin, place in a sieve and, using the back of a spoon, press out juices. Transfer pulp to a food processor or blender, add garlic, parsley, tahini (sesame seed paste) and lemon juice and process until smooth. Serve with pitta bread and vegetables.

MARINATED VEGETABLE SALAD

Garlic and Tahini Dip, Marinated Vegetable Salad

500 g/1 lb eggplant (aubergine), cut
into thick strips
salt
$^1/_2$ cup/125 mL/4 fl oz olive oil
$^1/_4$ cup/60 mL/2 fl oz white
wine vinegar
3 cloves garlic, crushed
2 teaspoons chopped fresh thyme or
$^1/_2$ teaspoon dried thyme
250 g/8 oz cherry tomatoes, halved
3 spring onions, sliced
freshly ground black pepper

1 Place eggplant (aubergine) strips in
a colander set over a bowl, sprinkle
with salt and stand for 15-20 minutes.
Rinse eggplant (aubergine) under cold
running water, drain well and pat dry
on absorbent kitchen paper.

2 Heat $^1/_4$ cup/60 mL/2 fl oz oil in a
large frying pan over a medium heat,
add eggplant (aubergine) and cook,
stirring occasionally, until golden.
Drain eggplant (aubergine) and place
in a serving bowl.

3 Place remaining oil, vinegar, garlic
and thyme in a screwtop jar and shake
well to combine. Pour over eggplant
(aubergine) and toss to combine. Cover
and marinate at room temperature for
at least 1 hour.

4 To serve, add tomatoes and spring
onions to eggplant (aubergine)
mixture, toss to combine and season
to taste with black pepper.

Serves 6

This salad will make an
interesting addition to an
antipasto platter. Its also a
delicious topper for toasted
garlic foccacia.

TOMATO SOUFFLES

Oven temperature
200°C, 400°F, Gas 6

Choose smooth, well-formed tomatoes that are heavy for their size. Buy bright-red tomatoes for immediate use and green to pale-pink tomatoes for future use, as tomatoes continue to ripen after harvest.

6 tomatoes
salt
15 g/^{1}/$_2$ oz butter
1 tablespoon flour
^{1}/$_2$ cup/125 mL/4 fl oz milk
2 teaspoons Dijon mustard
3 eggs separated

1   Cut tops from tomatoes and scoop out flesh. Sprinkle tomato shells lightly with salt, invert on absorbent kitchen paper and set aside to drain for 20 minutes.

2   Melt butter in a saucepan over a medium heat, add flour and cook, stirring, for 1 minute. Remove pan from heat and gradually whisk in milk, then

mustard. Return pan to heat and cook, stirring constantly, for 3-4 minutes or until sauce boils and thickens. Remove pan from heat and set aside to cool slightly.

3   Whisk egg yolks into sauce. Place egg whites in a clean bowl and beat until stiff peaks form. Fold egg whites into sauce.

4   Spoon soufflé mixture into tomato shells, place in a lightly greased baking dish and bake for 20 minutes or until soufflés are puffed and golden. Serve immediately.

Serves 6

TOMATO TRIANGLES

Oven temperature
180°C, 350°F, Gas 4

Ripen unripe tomatoes, stem down, not touching each other, at room temperature, out of direct sunlight, until bright red and slightly soft. Ripe tomatoes can be refrigerated for up to a week. Their flavour will improve if removed from refrigerator an hour before using.

500 g/1 lb tomatoes, peeled and finely chopped
4 spring onions, chopped
125 g/4 oz mozzarella cheese, grated
1 tablespoon chopped fresh oregano or
1 teaspoon dried oregano
freshly ground black pepper
10 sheets filo pastry
90 g/3 oz butter, melted
1 tablespoon sesame seeds

1   Combine tomatoes, spring onions, mozzarella cheese, oregano and black pepper to taste in a bowl.

2   Working with one sheet of pastry at a time, brush with melted butter and cut lengthwise into 3 pieces. Place 1 tablespoon tomato mixture on the corner of one short end, fold opposite corner up over filling to form a triangle enclosing the filling and continue folding to the end of the strip. Repeat with remaining pastry and filling.

3   Place triangles on a lightly greased baking tray, brush with remaining butter, sprinkle with sesame seeds and bake for 15 minutes or until golden.

Makes 30

Mediterranean Tomato Soup

Mediterranean Tomato Soup

45 g/1¹/₂ oz butter
2 tablespoons olive oil
2 carrots, finely diced
2 stalks celery, diced
1 leek, sliced
1 clove garlic, crushed
1.5 kg/3 lb tomatoes, peeled and chopped
3 tablespoons chopped fresh basil or coriander
1¹/₂ tablespoons sugar
freshly ground black pepper
freshly grated Parmesan cheese

1   Heat butter and oil in a saucepan over a medium heat, add carrots, celery, leek and garlic and cook, stirring, for 10 minutes or until vegetables are just tender.

2   Add tomatoes, basil or coriander and sugar to pan and bring to the boil. Reduce heat, cover and simmer for 30 minutes or until mixture thickens. Season to taste with black pepper. Ladle into soup bowls and sprinkle with Parmesan cheese.

Serves 8

Use tomatoes at their peak of ripeness in this soup to achieve the best flavour. To peel tomatoes, nick skin several times and place in a bowl. Pour over boiling water to cover and leave for 30 seconds. Drain, plunge into iced water and peel away skin.

STALKS AND SHOOTS

Served lightly cooked, crisp and either hot or cold, fresh garden greens like asparagus, celery, fennel, silverbeet (Swiss chard) and young spinach are delicious and versatile. They fit well into any meal – as appetisers, first courses, salads and main dishes.

TASTY FRESH ASPARAGUS

When buying asparagus, choose firm, brittle spears that are bright green in colour with tightly closed tips. The diameter of the stalk has no relationship to tenderness. Spears should be at least two-thirds green. To store, wrap ends in damp absorbent kitchen paper or stand in a container in 1 cm/$^1/_2$ in water, cover with a plastic food bag and store in the refrigerator.

250 g/8 oz asparagus

ACCOMPANIMENTS
3 tablespoons mayonnaise mixed with 2 teaspoons Dijon mustard or melted butter and freshly ground black pepper or freshly grated Parmesan cheese or a squeeze of lemon or lime juice

1   Snap off and discard tough ends of asparagus. If desired, peel stalks using a vegetable peeler. Plunge into cold water, remove and drain.

2   Boil, steam or microwave asparagus until just tender – take care not to overcook. Transfer to serving plate and serve plain or with one of the suggested accompaniments.

Serves 2

Tasty Fresh Asparagus

ASPARAGUS AND TROUT CROUTES

Oven temperature
200°C, 400°F, Gas 6

250 g/8 oz prepared puff pastry
1 egg yolk, lightly beaten
250 g/8 oz asparagus

HORSERADISH CREAM FILLING
15 g/^{1}/$_2$ oz butter
1 onion, finely chopped
1 cup/250 mL/8 fl oz cream (double)
^{1}/$_4$ cup/60 mL/2 fl oz dry white wine
1 tablespoon horseradish cream
250 g/8 oz smoked trout, boned
and flaked
1 tablespoon snipped fresh dill

The Greek word
'aspharagos', from which
asparagus derives, means
as long as one's throat!

1   Roll out pastry to 3 mm/^{1}/$_8$ in thick
and, using an 8 cm/3^1/$_4$ in cutter, cut
into eight rounds. Brush each round
lightly with egg yolk. Place four pastry
rounds on a baking tray and top with
remaining rounds. Bake for 12-15
minutes or until pastry is puffed and
golden. Set aside and keep warm.

2   Trim asparagus stems. Blanch in a
saucepan of boiling water for 1 minute,
drain and plunge into cold water to
stop the cooking process, then drain
again. Cut into 3 cm/1^1/$_4$ in lengths
and set aside.

3   To make filling, melt butter in a
saucepan over a medium heat, add
onion and cook, stirring, for 2 minutes
or until onion is soft. Stir in cream,
wine and horseradish cream, bring to
the boil then reduce heat and simmer,
stirring constantly, for 5 minutes or
until sauce thickens and is glossy. Add
asparagus, trout and dill to sauce and
heat for 2-3 minutes.

4   To assemble, split pastry rounds and
place bottom halves on serving plates.
Top with filling and cover with pastry
tops. Serve immediately.

Serves 4

CELERY IN OYSTER SAUCE

Left: Asparagus and Trout Croûtes
Above: Celery in Oyster Sauce

$^1/_2$ cup/125 mL/4 fl oz chicken stock
1 bunch celery, cut into thin
10 cm/4 in strips
1 tablespoon oyster sauce

Place stock in a frying pan and bring to the boil over a medium heat. Add celery, reduce heat, cover and simmer for 5 minutes. Using a slotted spoon, remove celery from pan and arrange on a serving platter. Stir oyster sauce into stock. Spoon stock mixture over celery. Serve immediately.

Serves 6

One of the best ways to cook celery is to lightly braise it in stock. Be sure to serve the cooking liquid with the celery to enjoy the fullest flavour.

CELERY COCKTAIL BITES

6 stalks celery
125 g/4 oz blue vein cheese
125 g/4 oz ricotta cheese
freshly ground black pepper
$^1/_4$ red pepper, cut into thin slivers
(optional)

Celery can be considered a total vegetable since all parts are edible (stalks, heart and leaves). Stringless varieties are also now available.

1 Remove a thin slice from the back of each celery stalk so that it sits flat when placed with the edges up.

2 Place blue vein and ricotta cheese in a bowl and mix until smooth. Spoon or pipe mixture into celery. Sprinkle with black pepper to taste and cut into 3 cm/1$^1/_4$ in lengths. Garnish with red pepper slivers (if using).

Makes 36

FENNEL AND POTATO SALAD

1 kg/2 lb small new potatoes
1 tablespoon olive oil
750 g/1$^1/_2$ lb fennel bulbs, cut into
wedges, reserve leaves
$^1/_4$ cup/60 mL/2 fl oz water
$^1/_3$ cup/90 mL/3 fl oz lemon juice
2 teaspoons wholegrain mustard
$^1/_2$ red pepper, thinly sliced

Look for firm, crisp, white bulbs with rigid stalks and feathery, bright-green leaves. Refrigerate unwashed in a plastic food bag for up to a week. To prepare, trim off stalks and base and remove any outer leaves that are loose. Rinse well, cut lengthwise into halves or quarters, dice, slice or cut into thin strips and use as desired.

1 Place potatoes in a saucepan, cover with cold water and bring to the boil over a medium heat. Reduce heat and simmer for 6-8 minutes or until potatoes are just tender, drain and place in a heatproof serving bowl.

2 Heat oil in a frying pan over a medium heat, add fennel and cook, stirring, for 2-3 minutes or until fennel starts to brown. Pour water over fennel, cover and cook for 5-8 minutes or until tender. Remove fennel from pan, leaving liquid. Add fennel to potatoes and lightly toss to combine.

3 Stir lemon juice, mustard and red pepper into the frying pan, bring to simmering and simmer until mixture reduces by half. Drizzle hot lemon mixture over fennel and potatoes and garnish with fennel leaves. Serve hot or cold.

Serves 8

Fennel and Ham Gnocchi

FENNEL AND HAM GNOCCHI

1 kg/2 lb gnocchi
1 tablespoon olive oil
1 clove garlic, crushed
500 g/1 lb fennel bulbs, chopped,
reserve leaves
200 g/6$^{1}/_{2}$ oz ham, cut into
5 cm/2 in long strips
1$^{1}/_{4}$ cups/315 mL/10 fl oz cream
(double)
1$^{1}/_{2}$ tablespoons tomato paste (purée)
freshly ground black pepper
grated fresh Parmesan cheese

1   Cook gnocchi in boiling water in a large saucepan following packet directions. Drain, set aside and keep warm.

2   Heat oil in a frying pan over a medium heat, add garlic, fennel and ham and cook, stirring, for 5 minutes or until fennel is just tender. Add cream and tomato paste (purée) and cook, stirring, for 2-3 minutes.

3   Add cooked gnocchi to sauce, season to taste with black pepper and heat for 2-3 minutes. Sprinkle with Parmesan cheese and chopped fennel leaves and serve.

Serves 6

Gnocchi is available from Italian delicatessens and some supermarkets or you can make your own.
To make gnocchi, mash 500 g/1 lb cooked potatoes until smooth. Add 2 eggs and 1 cup/125 g/4 oz flour and mix to make a stiff dough. Shape small spoonfuls of mixture into oval shapes and cook in boiling water for 3 minutes or until they rise to the surface.
Fennel is sometimes called anise due to its mild aniseed flavour.

Above: Fish and Vegetable Rolls
Right: Spinach Roulade

FISH AND VEGETABLE ROLLS

6 x 155 g/5 oz boneless thin white fish fillets
2 tablespoons finely grated fresh ginger
2 teaspoons finely chopped fresh thyme or $^1/_2$ teaspoon dried thyme
freshly ground black pepper
1 carrot, cut into thin strips
1 lemon, thinly peeled and rind cut into thin strips
6 silverbeet (Swiss chard) leaves, stalks removed
soy sauce

Silverbeet (also known as Swiss chard) has large, firm, strongly veined, deep-green glossy leaves and a long, white, fleshy stalk. Often wrongly called 'spinach', silverbeet has its own distinctive texture and a stronger flavour. Spinach could be used in this recipe if you wish, however you will need to choose large leaves or overlap several to make a covering big enough for the parcels.

1   Sprinkle fish fillets with ginger, thyme and black pepper to taste. Divide carrot and lemon rind strips into six bundles, place one bundle at the narrow end of each fillet and roll up fish to encase the bundle.

2   Wrap each fish roll in a silverbeet (Swiss chard) leaf to form a parcel. Secure with string. Place parcels in a steamer set over a saucepan of simmering water, cover and cook for 15 minutes or until fish is cooked. Serve with soy sauce.

Serves 6

SPINACH ROULADE

1 bunch/500 g/1 lb spinach
4 eggs, separated
2 tablespoons flour
3 tablespoons chopped fresh basil or
1 teaspoon dried basil leaves
$^1/_2$ teaspoon freshly grated nutmeg
375 g/12 oz ricotta cheese
$^1/_4$ red pepper, chopped
freshly ground black pepper

1   Rinse spinach in cold water, drain and place in a saucepan over a medium heat, cover and cook for 2 minutes or until just tender. Drain well and squeeze to remove excess liquid. Place in a food processor or blender, process to make a purée.

2   Place spinach, egg yolks, flour, basil and nutmeg in a bowl and mix to combine. Place egg whites in a clean bowl and beat until stiff peaks form. Fold egg whites into spinach mixture.

3   Pour spinach mixture into a greased and lined 26 x 32 cm/10$^1/_2$ x 12$^3/_4$ in Swiss roll tin and bake for 10 minutes or until cooked. Turn roulade onto a damp teatowel and peel away paper. Roll up in teatowel and set aside to cool.

4   Place ricotta cheese in a bowl and beat until smooth. Unroll roulade and spread with ricotta cheese, sprinkle with red pepper and black pepper to taste and roll up tightly. Cover and refrigerate for 30 minutes or until firm. To serve, cut into slices.

Serves 6

Oven temperature
180°C, 350°F, Gas 4

Select spinach bunches that have crisp, tender, clean, bright-green leaves. Avoid those with yellow, spotted or wilted leaves.

27

BEANS, PEAS & SWEET CORN

Probably the three most favourite vegetables on any family's wish list are corn-on-the-cob, green beans and shelled baby peas. Bean sprouts and tender snow peas (mangetout), both new guises of old favourites, fall not too far behind. All are sweet and delicious whether served traditionally or in trendy new salads and stir-fries.

CORN WITH HAM AND MUSHROOMS
Microwave

90 g/3 oz ham, finely diced
$^{1}/_{2}$ red pepper, finely diced
60 g/2 oz butter, softened
4 cobs sweet corn, husks and
silk removed
125 g/4 oz button mushrooms, sliced

1 Place ham, red pepper and butter in a bowl and mix well to combine. Spread one quarter of the mixture over each cob of sweet corn. Place each cob on a square of microwavable plastic food wrap, top with sliced mushrooms, then wrap to completely enclose.

2 Cook on HIGH (100%) for 8-10 minutes or until cooked. Alternatively the corn can be cooked on the barbecue or baked. Follow the instructions above but wrap in foil and cook in oven at 180°C/350°F/Gas 4 or on a preheated medium barbecue for 15-18 minutes.

Serves 4

Select fresh-looking cobs of corn that have green husks, moist stems and silk ends and those that are free of decay or worm injury. A simple test to assess freshness is to pierce a kernel with a thumbnail which should produce a spurt of milky juice. Avoid dry, shrivelled husks, immature white kernels or cobs with missing kernels.

Corn with Ham and Mushrooms

CORN AND CLAM CHOWDER

45 g/1¹/₂ oz butter
1 stalk celery, chopped
1 onion, finely chopped
2 potatoes, diced
1 tablespoon flour
440 g/14 oz canned chicken
consommé
1 cup/250 mL/8 fl oz cream (double)
1 cup/250 mL/8 fl oz milk
3 cobs sweet corn, kernels removed or
315 g/10 oz canned sweet corn
kernels, drained
280 g/9 oz canned baby clams, drained

1   Melt butter in a large saucepan over a medium heat, add celery, onion and potatoes and cook, stirring, for 2 minutes or until onion is tender.

2   Add flour to pan and cook, stirring, for 1 minute. Remove pan from heat and gradually stir in consommé, cream and milk. Return pan to heat and cook, stirring constantly, for 5-7 minutes or until soup boils and thickens.

3   Stir sweet corn into soup, reduce heat, cover and simmer for 15 minutes or until corn is tender. Add clams and cook for 2-3 minutes longer.

Serves 6

Sweet corn is best eaten as soon as possible after havesting. The fresher the corn the sweeter the flavour. If stored, the sugar content quickly turns to starch at higher temperatures.

RED KIDNEY AND GREEN BEAN RICE

45 g/1¹/₂ oz butter
2 cloves garlic, crushed
1 onion, chopped
440 g/14 oz white rice
4 cups/1 litre/1³/₄ pt chicken stock
315 g/10 oz canned red kidney beans,
rinsed and drained
500 g/1 lb green beans, cut into
5 mm/¹/₄ in pieces

1   Melt butter in a large saucepan over a medium heat, add garlic and onion and cook, stirring, for 5 minutes or until onion is tender. Add rice and cook, stirring constantly, for 2 minutes or until rice is well coated.

2   Stir stock into rice mixture, cover and bring to the boil. Reduce heat and simmer for 10 minutes. Stir red kidney beans and green beans into pan, cover and cook for 5 minutes or until liquid is absorbed and rice and green beans are tender. Serve hot or cold.

Serves 8

Choose slender, crisp beans that are bright in colour and blemish free. Avoid mature beans with large seeds and swollen pods. Good beans will snap readily when broken.

Bean and Melon Salad

Bean and Melon Salad

250 g/8 oz fine green beans
1 honeydew melon, halved and seeded
4 hard-boiled eggs, cut into wedges
155 g/5 oz cherry tomatoes, halved

SWEET MUSTARD DRESSING
$^1/_2$ cup/125 mL/4 fl oz olive oil
$^1/_4$ cup/60 mL/2 fl oz vinegar
2 tablespoons wholegrain mustard
1 tablespoon caster sugar

1 Boil, steam or microwave beans until just tender, plunge into cold water to stop the cooking process. Drain on absorbent kitchen paper.

2 Using a melon baller, scoop balls of melon from melon halves and place in a salad bowl. Add beans, eggs and tomatoes.

3 To make dressing, place oil, vinegar, mustard and sugar in a screwtop jar and shake well to combine. Drizzle dressing over salad and toss to combine.

Serves 6

The two main types of fresh beans are the common green bean (also known as French beans) and runner beans (or climbing beans), which are sometimes called butter beans. Some varieties produce yellow wax beans, stringless beans or purple beans – which turn green when cooked!

Above: Spicy Indian Beans
Right: Chicken and Sprout Salad

SPICY INDIAN BEANS

2 tablespoons olive oil
$^1/_2$ teaspoon fennel seeds
$^1/_2$ teaspoon ground turmeric
$^1/_2$ teaspoon finely grated fresh ginger
1 fresh red chilli, seeded and chopped
2 potatoes, diced
500 g/1 lb green beans, cut into
2.5-5 cm/1-2 in lengths
2 tablespoons lemon juice

To store beans, refrigerate unwashed, in a plastic food bag or container. To prepare beans for cooking, simply wash, then top and tail.

Heat oil in a large frying pan over a medium heat, add fennel seeds, turmeric, ginger and chilli and cook, stirring, for 1 minute or until fragrant. Add potatoes and cook, stirring for 2 minutes. Add beans to pan and cook for 2 minutes longer. Add lemon juice, cover and simmer for 8 minutes or until vegetables are just tender. Serve hot or cold.

Serves 6

CHICKEN AND SPROUT SALAD

assorted lettuce leaves
250 g/8 oz bean sprouts
45 g/1½ oz snow pea (mangetout)
sprouts or watercress
250 g/8 oz smoked chicken, cut
into thin strips
125 g/4 oz yellow teardrop tomatoes,
halved or 1 yellow tomato, cut into
thin wedges
1 pomegranate, seeds removed, or
90 g/3 oz fresh red currants

LEMON MINT DRESSING
3 tablespoons olive oil
2 tablespoons lemon juice
1 tablespoon chopped fresh mint
freshly ground black pepper

1   Line a salad bowl with lettuce leaves
and arrange bean sprouts and snow pea
(mangetout) sprouts or watercress,
smoked chicken and tomatoes over
lettuce. Sprinkle pomegranate seeds or
currants over salad.

2   To make dressing, combine oil,
lemon juice, mint and black pepper to
taste in a screwtop jar and shake well to
combine. Drizzle dressing over salad
and serve.

Serves 6

A classic ingredient in Asian
cookery, sprouts are
generally grown from
golden soy, mung or curd
beans, however snow pea
(mangetout) sprouts are
now available from green
grocers and speciality food
markets.

GINGERED PRAWNS

1 tablespoon olive oil
1 teaspoon sesame oil
2 cloves garlic, crushed
1 teaspoon finely grated fresh ginger
625 g/1¼ lb uncooked prawns,
shelled and deveined, tails left intact
250 g/8 oz bean sprouts
8 spring onions, chopped
6 oyster mushrooms, sliced
1 tablespoon oyster sauce

Heat olive and sesame oils in a wok or large frying pan over a medium heat, add garlic, ginger and prawns and stir-fry for 2 minutes or until prawns change colour. Add bean sprouts, spring onions, mushrooms and oyster sauce and stir-fry for 4 minutes longer or until prawns are cooked and mixture is heated through. Serve immediately.

Serves 6

LAMB PIES WITH FRESH PEAS

2 tablespoons olive oil
2 onions, chopped
1½ teaspoons curry powder
750 g/1½ lb lean minced lamb
½ cup/125 mL/4 fl oz beef stock or
red wine
750 g/1½ lb peas in pods, shelled or
300 g/9½ oz shelled peas
½ cup/125 mL/4 fl oz cream (double)
1 tablespoon chopped fresh coriander
or mint
1 tablespoon fruit chutney
freshly ground black pepper
250 g/8 oz prepared puff pastry
1 egg yolk

1 Heat oil in a frying pan over a medium heat, add onions and curry powder and cook, stirring, for 5 minutes or until onions are soft. Add lamb to pan and cook for 4-5 minutes or until lamb is brown. Add stock or wine to pan, bring to simmering, cover and simmer for 15 minutes or until lamb is just tender.

2 Add peas, cream, coriander or mint, chutney and black pepper to taste to lamb mixture and cook uncovered, stirring occasionally, for 5 minutes or until peas are just tender and mixture thickens. Remove pan from heat and spoon mixture into six 1 cup/250 mL/ 8 fl oz capacity ramekins. Set aside to cool.

3 Roll out pastry to 3 mm/⅛ in thick and, using a cutter 1 cm/½ in larger than the diameter of the ramekins, cut pastry into six rounds. Brush rims of ramekins with egg yolk, place pastry over ramekins and brush with remaining egg yolk. Bake for 15-20 minutes or until pastry is puffed and golden.

Serves 6

Pea and Sweet Corn Hot Pot

Pea and Sweet Corn Hot Pot

15 g/$^1/_2$ oz butter
1 onion, chopped
500 g/1 lb peas in pods, shelled or
200 g/6$^1/_2$ oz shelled peas
1 cob sweet corn, kernels only or
125 g/4 oz canned sweet corn kernels,
drained
1$^1/_2$ tablespoons flour
1 cup/250 mL/8 fl oz milk
pinch ground paprika
freshly ground black pepper

Melt butter in a saucepan over a medium heat, add onion, peas and sweet corn and cook, stirring, for 2 minutes or until onion is soft. Stir flour into pan, cook, stirring, for 1 minute, remove pan from heat and gradually stir in milk, paprika and black pepper to taste. Return pan to heat and cook, stirring constantly, until mixture boils and thickens. Reduce heat, simmer for 2 minutes longer or until vegetables are just tender.

Serves 4

Look for peas that are crisp and have shiny, bright-green pods. Refrigerate unwashed in a plastic food bag. Split pea pods, remove peas and rinse before cooking.

35

HONEYED SCALLOPS AND PEAS

1 tablespoon vegetable oil
1 clove garlic, crushed
200 g/6^1/$_2$ oz snow peas (mangetout)
1 red pepper, cut into thin strips
2 tablespoons honey
100 g/3^1/$_2$ oz bean sprouts
250 g/8 oz scallops
1 teaspoon cornflour blended with
2 tablespoons water

1   Heat oil in a wok or large frying pan over a medium heat, add garlic, snow peas (mangetout) and red pepper and stir-fry for 1-2 minutes or until snow peas (mangetout) change colour.

2   Add honey, bean sprouts and scallops to pan and stir-fry for 2 minutes or until scallops are opaque. Stir in cornflour mixture, bring to the boil and cook until mixture thickens. Serve immediately.

Serves 4

Snow peas (mangetout) are edible pods that are renowned for their bright colour, delicate sweet flavour and crisp texture. These Oriental peas are wider and thinner than other peas.

SUMMER PEA AND PINE NUT SALAD

155 g/5 oz snow peas (mangetout)
1 bunch rocket or watercress
2 tomatoes, chopped
1 onion, finely chopped
30 g/1 oz pine nuts, toasted

BASIL DRESSING
3 tablespoons chopped fresh basil
3 tablespoons olive oil
1 tablespoon vinegar
1 clove garlic, crushed
freshly ground black pepper

1   Boil, steam or microwave snow peas (mangetout) until they just change colour. Refresh under cold running water.

2   Place snow peas (mangetout), rocket or watercress, tomatoes, onions and pine nuts in a salad bowl and toss to combine.

3   To make dressing, place basil, oil, vinegar, garlic and black pepper to taste in a screwtop jar and shake well to combine. Drizzle dressing over salad, toss and serve.

Serves 4

Choose snow peas (mangetout) that are crisp and bright green in colour. Avoid those that have brown spots or are wrinkly.

Minted Pea and Apple Salad

MINTED PEA AND APPLE SALAD

2 red apples, cored and thinly sliced
$^1/_4$ cup/60 mL/2 fl oz lemon juice
200 g/6$^1/_2$ oz snow peas (mangetout),
blanched
30 g/1 oz snow pea (mangetout)
sprouts or bean sprouts
$^1/_4$ cup/60 mL/2 fl oz olive oil
2 teaspoons chopped fresh mint
freshly ground black pepper

1 Place apples in a bowl, add lemon juice and toss to coat. Drain apples and reserve lemon juice. Place apples, snow peas (mangetout) and sprouts in a salad bowl and toss well to combine.

2 Place reserved lemon juice, oil, mint and black pepper to taste in a screwtop jar and shake well to combine. Drizzle dressing over salad, toss and serve.

Serves 6

Top and tail snow peas (mangetout) and remove the string that runs down both sides. To blanch, place in a saucepan of boiling water and cook for 20 seconds, drain, then plunge into cold water to stop the cooking process. Drain and pat dry on absorbent kitchen paper.

THE ONION FAMILY

It's difficult to ignore this family. The onion and its siblings (spring onions, leeks, garlic and chives) are the flavoursome base or rich seasoning for just about any other food you can imagine. But here, onions take centre stage in recipes for soups, pasta, pizza and interesting accompaniments.

MARINATED SALMON AND ONIONS

500 g/1 lb salmon fillets, thinly sliced
6 spring onions, finely chopped
2 cloves garlic, crushed
1/2 cup/125 mL/4 fl oz red
wine vinegar
1/4 cup/60 mL/2 fl oz olive oil
2 tablespoons chopped fresh mint
freshly ground black pepper
6 spring onions, cut into
12.5 cm/5 in lengths

1 Place salmon, chopped spring onions, garlic, vinegar, oil, mint and black pepper to taste in a shallow glass or ceramic dish, toss to combine, cover and marinate in the refrigerator for 2-3 hours.

2 Blanch remaining spring onions in a saucepan of boiling water for 1 minute, remove, plunge into cold water and drain.

3 Remove salmon from marinade, drain well and arrange on a serving platter. Garnish with blanched spring onions and chill until ready to serve.

Serves 6

Sometimes called green onions or scallions, spring onions are essentially onions harvested when very young. This easy dish is delicious as a light meal or first course of a special dinner party.

Sun-dried Tomato Pasta

SUN-DRIED TOMATO PASTA

250 g/8 oz bow-shaped pasta
15 g/^{1}/$_2$ oz butter
1 tablespoon olive oil
^{1}/$_2$ bunch spring onions, cut into
2 cm/^{3}/$_4$ in lengths
2 tablespoons brandy or dry sherry
1^1/$_4$ cups/315 mL/10 fl oz cream
(double)
6 sun-dried tomatoes, sliced
grated fresh Parmesan cheese
freshly ground black pepper

1   Cook pasta in boiling water in a large saucepan following packet directions. Drain, set aside and keep warm.

2   Heat butter and oil in a frying pan over a medium heat, add spring onions and cook, stirring, for 1 minute or until onions are soft. Stir in brandy or sherry, cream and sun-dried tomatoes, bring to simmering and simmer for 4-5 minutes or until sauce reduces and thickens.

3   Pour sauce over pasta and toss to combine. Sprinkle with Parmesan cheese and black pepper to taste. Serve immediately.

Serves 4

Choose spring onions with crisp, bright-green tops and clean white bottoms. Refrigerate unwashed. Store in a plastic food bag or wrap in plastic food wrap.

PROVENÇAL ONIONS

^{1}/4 cup/60 mL/2 fl oz olive oil
1 kg/2 lb pickling or small onions,
peeled
750 g/1 ^{1}/2 lb tomatoes, chopped
90 g/3 oz sultanas
^{1}/3 cup/90 mL/3 fl oz vinegar
3 cloves garlic, crushed
3 tablespoons chopped fresh basil
1 tablespoon sugar
freshly ground black pepper

Pickling onions are small white onions sometimes called pearl onions. They are firmer and sweeter than mature white onions which make them the perfect choice for tasty accompaniments such as this. When unavailable, substitute with the rounded bulbs of more mature spring onions.

1   Heat oil in a large frying pan over a medium heat, add onions and cook, stirring, for 3-4 minutes or until onions are golden. Add tomatoes, sultanas, vinegar, garlic, basil and sugar and mix to combine.

2   Bring mixture to the boil, reduce heat, cover and simmer for 30 minutes. Uncover and cook for 30 minutes longer or until sauce reduces and thickens and onions are tender. Season to taste with black pepper. Serve hot or cold.

Serves 8

Left: Provençal Onions
Above: Onion Pitta Pizza

ONION PITTA PIZZA

$^1/_3$ cup/90 mL/3 fl oz olive oil
750 g/1 $^1/_2$ lb onions, thinly sliced
4 pitta bread rounds
$^1/_2$ cup/125 mL/4 fl oz prepared
tomato pasta sauce
4 black olives, pitted and sliced
4 sun-dried tomatoes, chopped
2 tablespoons chopped fresh basil or
$^1/_2$ teaspoon dried basil
125 g/4 oz mozzarella cheese, sliced

1   Heat oil in a frying pan over a medium heat, add onions and cook, stirring, for 10 minutes or until onions are tender and golden brown.

2   Place pitta bread on baking trays and spread evenly with pasta sauce. Top with onions, olives and sun-dried tomatoes and sprinkle with basil and cheese. Bake for 10 minutes or until bread is crisp and cheese melts. To serve, cut into wedges.

Serves 4

Oven temperature
200°C, 400°F, Gas 6

Select firm, well-shaped onions which have small necks and dry, papery skin. Avoid spongy or sprouting onions with uneven or patchy skin colouring.

41

FRENCH ONION SOUP

45 g/1¹/₂ oz butter
1 clove garlic, crushed
4 onions, thinly sliced
¹/₄ cup/60 mL/2 fl oz sherry
2 x 440 g/14 oz canned beef consommé
2 cups/500 mL/16 fl oz water
¹/₂ teaspoon sugar
freshly ground black pepper
CROUTONS
1 bread stick, sliced
olive oil
grated fresh Parmesan cheese

1   Melt butter in a frying pan over a low heat, add garlic and onions and cook, stirring frequently, for 15-20 minutes or until onions are golden and tender.

2   Stir in sherry and cook over a medium heat for 1 minute or until sherry evaporates. Add consommé, water and sugar to pan, bring to the boil, then reduce heat, cover and simmer for 30 minutes. Season to taste with black pepper.

3   To make crôutons, brush bread with oil and cook under a preheated medium grill for 2-3 minutes each side or until golden. Sprinkle with Parmesan cheese and serve with soup.

Serves 6

Choose large, brown sweet mature onions for this recipe and cook them very slowly in step 1 until they almost caramelise to achieve the best flavour.

VICHYSSOISE

45 g/1¹/₂ oz butter
500 g/1 lb leeks, thinly sliced
500 g/1 lb potatoes, sliced
4 cups/1 litre/1³/₄ pt chicken stock
¹/₂ cup/125 mL/4 fl oz white wine
1 cup/250 mL/8 fl oz cream (double)
1 bunch fresh chives, snipped

1   Melt butter in a large saucepan over a medium heat, add leeks and cook, stirring, for 5 minutes or until leeks are just tender. Add potatoes, stock and wine to pan, bring to the boil, then reduce heat, cover and simmer for 10 minutes or until potatoes are tender.

2   Remove pan from heat and set aside to cool slightly. Place mixture, in batches, in a food processor or blender and process until smooth. Return soup to a clean saucepan, add cream and heat gently. Serve hot or very well chilled. Just prior to serving, garnish with chives.

Serves 6

Choose leeks no larger than 5 cm/2 in in diameter and trim off all but 5 cm/2 in of the green tops. The best way to wash leeks is to cut them in half lengthwise and rinse halves under cold running water until all the grit is removed.

Leek and Bacon Quiche

LEEK AND BACON QUICHE

SHORTCRUST PASTRY
2 cups/250 g/8 oz flour
125 g/4 oz butter
2-3 tablespoons lemon juice

LEEK AND BACON FILLING
30g/1 oz butter
2 leeks, thinly sliced
125 g/4 oz bacon, chopped
60g/2 oz grated tasty cheese
(mature Cheddar)
2 eggs
$^1/_2$ cup/125 mL/4 fl oz cream (double)

1   Place flour and butter in a food processor and process until mixture resembles fine breadcrumbs. With machine running, add enough lemon juice to form a soft dough. Turn dough onto a lightly floured surface and knead briefly. Wrap in plastic food wrap and refrigerate for 30 minutes.

2   Roll out pastry to fit six 12 cm/ 5 in flan tins or one 25 cm/10 in flan tin with removable base. Line pastry with nonstick baking paper and fill with uncooked rice. Bake the small pastry cases for 12 minutes or the large case for 15-18 minutes. Remove rice and paper and set aside to cool.

3   To make filling, melt butter in a large frying pan over a medium heat, add leeks and bacon and cook, stirring, for 3-4 minutes or until leeks are golden. Spoon mixture into base of pastry case/s and sprinkle with cheese. Place eggs and cream in a bowl, mix to combine and pour over filling. Bake the small quiches for 20 minutes and the large quiche for 35 minutes or until cooked through and golden. Serve hot or cold.

Serves 6

Oven temperature
200°C, 400°F, Gas 6

Select leeks with clean, crisp, white bottoms and fresh-looking tops. Small to medium-size leeks are the most tender with a mild, delicate flavour.

ROOTS AND TUBERS

Some roots and tubers like radishes, swedes, celeriac and kohlrabi have distinctly earthy flavours that hold their own with a variety of strong seasonings. Others like carrots, parsnips, beetroot and Jerusalem artichokes, are sweet and mild, especially when young. Treat them all with a minimum of fuss to enjoy economical vegetables at their very best.

RADISH CREAM DRESSING

$^1/_2$ cup/125 mL/4 fl oz cream (double)
$^1/_2$ cup/125 g/4 oz sour cream
3 tablespoons snipped fresh chives
freshly ground black pepper
12 radishes, grated

Place cream, sour cream, chives and black pepper to taste in a bowl and stir to combine. Stir radishes into mixture. Chill until required. Serve over baked or boiled potatoes or as an accompaniment to grilled meats.

Serves 8

Select radishes that are crisp, bright and heavy for their size, with fresh-looking leaves.

Radish Cream Dressing

Sweet Radish and Pea Salad

12 radishes, sliced
100 g/3^1/$_2$ oz snow peas (mangetout)
SWEET SESAME DRESSING
1 tablespoon caster sugar
2 tablespoons white vinegar
1 tablespoon soy sauce
1 teaspoon sesame oil

1   To make dressing, place sugar, vinegar, soy sauce and sesame oil in a screwtop jar and shake well to combine.

2   Place radishes and snow peas (mangetout) in a salad bowl. Spoon over dressing and toss to combine. Set aside to stand for 30 minutes, then toss again before serving.

Serves 6

Refrigerate radishes in a plastic food bag if you intend to store for longer than 2-3 days; radishes will keep better if leaves are removed.

Radish Leaf Soup

45 g/1^1/$_2$ oz butter
1 onion, chopped
250 g/8 oz potatoes, diced
leaves from 12 radishes
2 x 440 g/14 oz canned chicken consommé or 6 cups/1.5 litres/ 2^1/$_2$ pt chicken stock
^{1}/$_2$ cup/125 mL/4 fl oz cream (double)
freshly ground black pepper

1   Melt butter in a saucepan over a medium heat, add onion and potatoes and cook, stirring, for 4-5 minutes or until onion is golden. Add radish leaves and consommé or stock and bring to the boil. Reduce heat, cover and simmer for 15 minutes or until potatoes are tender. Remove pan from heat and set aside to cool slightly.

2   Transfer mixture, in batches, to a food processor or blender and process until smooth. Return soup to a clean saucepan, stir cream into mixture and heat gently. Season to taste with black pepper and serve.

Serves 8

This soup is essentially a Vichyssoise with the satisfying 'bite' of radishes. Use only the freshest unblemished leaves for the best results.

Baby Beets with Yogurt

BABY BEETS WITH YOGURT

12 small beetroot

YOGURT CHIVE DRESSING
250 g/8 oz natural yogurt
2 tablespoons snipped fresh chives
1 teaspoon finely grated lemon rind
freshly ground black pepper

1 Cut off all but 3 cm/1^1/4 in of the
stalk from each beetroot and discard.
Place beetroot in a saucepan of cold
water and bring to the boil. Reduce
heat and simmer for 15 minutes or until
tender. Drain and cool slightly. Trim
tops and tails and remove skins from
beetroot. Place beetroot in a serving bowl.

2 To make dressing, combine yogurt,
chives, lemon rind and black pepper to
taste in a bowl and mix well to
combine. Serve beetroot hot or cold
accompanied by dressing.

Serves 6

Beetroot can be used to
enhance many 'non-beet'
recipes. For example, a
small beetroot added to
apples when stewing will
give them a rosy glow.

BEETROOT SOUP

Another simple way to enjoy beets is to slice them after cooking and serve cold as a salad with a dressing of sour cream and chopped fresh mint or dill.

4 beetroot, grated
2 carrots, grated
1 onion, grated
4 cups/1 litre/1³/4 pt chicken stock
4 tablespoons snipped fresh dill
1 tablespoon lemon juice
freshly ground black pepper

Place beetroot, carrots, onion, stock, dill and lemon juice in a saucepan and bring to the boil over a medium heat. Reduce heat, cover and simmer for 15 minutes or until vegetables are tender. Season to taste with black pepper. Serve hot or well chilled.

Serves 8

CARAWAY BEETROOT WITH BACON

Select beetroot with smooth, firm roots and good colour. The freshness of the leaves is no indication of the quality of the roots. Avoid soft, flabby, tough or woody beets. Trim stems leaving 3 cm/1¹/4 in intact. Refrigerate in a plastic food bag for up to a week.

1 tablespoon olive oil
250 g/8 oz bacon, chopped
1 clove garlic, crushed
4 beetroot, grated
¹/2 cup/125 mL/4 fl oz orange juice
1 teaspoon caraway seeds

1   Heat oil in a frying pan over a medium heat, add bacon and garlic and cook, stirring, for 3-4 minutes or until bacon is crisp.

2   Stir beetroot, orange juice and caraway seeds into pan and cook for 2-3 minutes or until beetroot is just tender and juice almost evaporated. Serve immediately.

Serves 6

CARROT AND NUT MUFFINS

Carrot and Nut Muffins

500 g/1 lb carrots, chopped
125 g/4 oz butter
$^1/_2$ cup/100 g/3$^1/_2$ oz caster sugar
2 eggs
3 cups/375 g/12 oz self-raising flour
$^2/_3$ cup/155 g/5 oz sour cream
30 g/1 oz chopped nuts

1   Place carrots in a saucepan of boiling water and cook for 20 minutes or until carrots are tender. Drain and set aside to cool slightly. Place carrots in a food processor or blender, process until smooth and set aside.

2   Place butter and sugar in a bowl and beat until light and fluffy. Add eggs, one at a time, beating well after each addition. Stir flour, sour cream, carrot purée and nuts into egg mixture and mix to combine.

3   Spoon mixture into lightly greased 1 cup/250 mL/8 fl oz capacity muffin tins. Bake for 25-30 minutes or until muffins are cooked and golden. Serve hot, warm or cold.

Makes 12

Oven temperature
180°C, 350°F, Gas 4

Carrots are an excellent source of vitamin A and a good source of dietary fibre, calcium and phosphorus. The deeper the orange colour of a carrot, the higher the vitamin A content.

REFRESHING CARROT SOUP

15 g/^{1}/$_2$ oz butter
1 onion, chopped
500 g/1 lb carrots, chopped
4 cups/1 litre/1^3/$_4$ pt chicken stock
1 tablespoon chopped fresh mint or
coriander
1 teaspoon chopped fresh thyme or
^{1}/$_4$ teaspoon dried thyme
^{1}/$_4$ cup/60 mL/2 fl oz cream (double)

1   Melt butter in a large saucepan over a medium heat, add onion and cook, stirring, for 3 minutes or until onion is soft. Add carrots, stock, mint or coriander and thyme to pan and mix to combine.

2   Bring mixture to the boil, reduce heat, cover and simmer for 10 minutes or until carrots are tender. Remove pan from heat and set aside to cool slightly. Place mixture, in batches, in a food processor or blender and process until smooth. Return soup to a clean saucepan, stir in cream and heat gently.

Serves 4

Choose bright-coloured, firm, well-shaped carrots. When tops are still attached, look for fresh green leaves. Avoid dry, wilted, shrivelled, soft or split carrots.

HONEY GLAZED BABY CARROTS

15 g/^{1}/$_2$ oz butter
500 g/1 lb baby carrots, scrubbed
2 cloves garlic, crushed
1 tablespoon chopped fresh rosemary
leaves or 1 teaspoon dried rosemary
2 tablespoons honey
1 tablespoon white wine or apple juice

Melt butter in a frying pan over a medium heat, add carrots, garlic, rosemary, honey and wine or apple juice and mix to combine. Cover and cook, stirring occasionally, for 10 minutes or until carrots are just tender. Serve immediately.

Serves 6

It is not necessary to peel baby carrots. The tender skin is very sweet and rich in vitamins.

Parsnip and Salmon Tart

PARSNIP AND SALMON TART

250 g/8 oz prepared shortcrust pastry

PARSNIP AND SALMON FILLING
750 g/1½ lb parsnips, chopped
45 g/1½ oz walnuts, toasted and
roughly chopped
2 eggs
4 tablespoons snipped fresh chives
freshly ground black pepper
440 g/14 oz canned salmon, drained
and flaked
2 tablespoons mayonnaise

1   Roll out pastry to 3 mm/⅛ in thick
and use to line a 25 cm/10 in fluted flan
tin with a removable base. Line pastry
case with nonstick baking paper and fill
with uncooked rice. Bake for 12
minutes, then remove rice and paper
and set aside to cool.

2   To make filling, place parsnips in a
saucepan of boiling water and simmer
for 15 minutes or until tender. Drain
and set aside to cool slightly. Place
parsnips in a food processor or blender
and process until smooth. Place in a
bowl, add walnuts, eggs, chives and
black pepper to taste and mix to
combine. Place salmon and mayonnaise
in a separate bowl and mix to combine.

3   Spread half the parsnip mixture over
base of pastry case. Top with salmon
mixture, then remaining parsnip
mixture. Bake for 25-30 minutes or
until filling is firm to the touch. Serve
hot, warm or at room temperature.

Serves 12

Oven temperature
180°C, 350°F, Gas 4

The creamy-skinned parsnip
is cultivated for its large,
tapering, fleshy taproot
which has a delicate, nutty
flavour.

PARSNIPS AND PEARS

1 orange
15 g/^{1}/2 oz butter
1 tablespoon olive oil
500 g/1 lb parsnips, thickly sliced
2 pears, thinly sliced

1   Squeeze the juice from the orange and set aside. Remove membrane and pith from half the orange rind and cut rind into thin strips.

2   Heat butter and oil in a frying pan over a medium heat, add parsnips and cook, stirring, for 5 minutes or until just tender. Add pears, orange strips and orange juice and cook for 2 minutes or until pears are heated through and juice almost evaporated.

Serves 6

Select small to medium, well-shaped parsnips which have a smooth, firm surface. Avoid large parsnips as these tend to have a woody core. Parsnips which have straggly roots or are blemished should also be avoided.

PARSNIP AND CELERY SOUP

250 g/8 oz parsnips, chopped
250 g/8 oz celery, chopped
60 g/2 oz butter
^{1}/4 cup/30 g/1 oz flour
3 cups/750 mL/1^1/4 pt chicken stock
1 cup/250 mL/8 fl oz milk
freshly ground black pepper
1 avocado, stoned, peeled and sliced
(optional)

1   Place parsnips and celery in a saucepan of boiling water and simmer for 10-15 minutes or until vegetables are tender. Drain and set aside to cool slightly. Place vegetables, in batches, in a food processor or blender and process until smooth.

2   Melt butter in a clean saucepan over a medium heat, add flour and cook, stirring, for 1 minute. Remove pan from heat and gradually whisk in stock and milk. Return pan to heat, add vegetable purée and bring to the boil, stirring constantly. Reduce heat and simmer for 5 minutes or until heated through. Season to taste with black pepper. Serve garnished with avocado slices, if desired.

Serves 6

Trim and discard parsnip tops and root ends. Wash thoroughly or peel. Slice, dice, shred, cut into thin strips or leave whole. Parsnips can be boiled, fried, mashed, used in soups or casseroles and make excellent chips.

Chilli-Garlic Swede and Beef

CHILLI-GARLIC SWEDE AND BEEF

250 g/8 oz rump steak, thinly sliced
2 tablespoons soy sauce
1 tablespoon honey
1 teaspoon chilli garlic sauce
60 g/2 oz shelled fresh or frozen peas
1 tablespoon vegetable oil
500 g/1 lb swedes, cut into thin
7.5 cm/3 in strips
100 g/3¹/₂ oz young spinach, chopped

1   Place beef, soy sauce, honey and chilli garlic sauce in a bowl and mix to combine. Cover and set aside to marinate for 1 hour. If using fresh peas, blanch in a saucepan of boiling water for 1 minute, remove, plunge into cold water and set aside.

2   Heat oil in a wok or large frying pan over a medium heat, add beef mixture and swedes and stir-fry for 2-3 minutes or until beef is browned and cooked through. Add spinach and peas and stir-fry for 2 minutes longer or until spinach just wilts.

Serves 6

The Swede (Swedish turnip) is also known as the rutabaga and is the result of cross-breeding between a cabbage and a turnip. Unlike turnips, which store well for only brief periods, swedes will keep for several weeks if refrigerated.

SWEDE AND CHICKEN PASTIES

Oven temperature
180°C, 350°F, Gas 4

250 g/8 oz prepared puff pastry
1 egg yolk

SWEDE AND CHICKEN FILLING
250 g/8 oz swedes, diced
375 g/12 oz chicken, minced
6 spring onions, chopped
1 egg
1 tablespoon chopped fresh basil or
1 teaspoon dried basil
1 tablespoon milk
freshly ground black pepper

1   To make filling, place swedes, chicken, spring onions, egg, basil, milk and black pepper to taste in a bowl and mix well to combine.

2   Roll out pastry to 3 mm/^{1}/8 in thick and, using a 10 cm/4 in cutter, cut out eight rounds. Reserve pastry scraps. Spoon filling onto centre of each pastry round. Brush edges lightly with water and fold pastry over filling, pressing edges together to seal.

3   Place pasties on greased baking trays. Cut a small slit in the top of each pasty, decorate with remaining pastry scraps and brush with egg yolk. Bake for 18-20 minutes or until pastry is puffed and golden.

Serves 6

Choose firm, young, small to medium-sized swedes which are heavy for their size. Avoid those which are blemished or have moist spots. Tops should be bright and fresh looking.

SWEDE AND POTATO PATTIES

750 g/1^1/2 lb swedes, chopped
250 g/8 oz potatoes, chopped
1 egg
2 cups/250 g/8 oz flour
1 tablespoon chopped fresh herbs or
1 teaspoon dried mixed herbs
2 tablespoons sesame seeds
freshly ground black pepper
45 g/1^1/2 oz butter
2 tablespoons olive oil

1   Place swedes and potatoes in a saucepan of boiling water and simmer for 20 minutes or until vegetables are tender. Drain and set aside to cool slightly. Place vegetables in a food processor or blender and process until smooth. Transfer vegetable purée to a bowl, add egg, 1 cup/125 g/4 oz flour and herbs and mix well to combine.

2   Place remaining flour in a shallow dish, add sesame seeds and black pepper to taste and mix to combine. Spoon 3 tablespoons swede mixture onto flour mixture and, using floured hands, shape mixture into a patty, coating well. Repeat with remaining mixture to make twelve patties.

3   Heat butter and oil in a large frying pan over a medium heat and cook patties for 3 minutes each side, or until brown and crusty. Drain on absorbent kitchen paper. Serve hot.

Makes 12

Swedes have a pretty yellow colour that makes these patties look pretty on the plate.

Honey and Lemon Turnips

54

HONEY AND LEMON TURNIPS

12 baby turnips or
2 medium turnips, quartered
2 sprigs fresh thyme or $1/4$ teaspoon
dried thyme
1-2 cups/250-500 mL/8-16 fl oz
chicken stock
1 tablespoon honey
1 tablespoon lemon juice

1   Place turnips and thyme in a saucepan and pour over enough stock to cover. Bring to the boil over a medium heat, reduce heat, cover and simmer for 5 minutes, or until just tender. Drain turnips and return to saucepan.

2   Add honey and lemon juice, toss to coat, heat for 3-4 minutes and serve.

Serves 6

The turnip is an underrated vegetable. Both the green leafy top and purple-white lobe-shaped root are edible and have a sweet to hot flavour, reminiscent of mustard.

TURNIP PATTIES WITH CHIVES

500 g/1 lb turnips, grated
$^3/_4$ cup/185 mL/6 fl oz milk
1 egg
$^1/_3$ cup/45 g/1$^1/_2$ oz flour
3 tablespoons snipped fresh chives
freshly ground black pepper
45 g/1$^1/_2$ oz butter
1 tablespoon olive oil

1   Place turnips, milk, egg, flour, chives and black pepper to taste in a bowl and mix well to combine.

2   Heat butter and oil in a frying pan over a medium heat. Shape 3 tablespoons of the turnip mixture into a patty and cook for 4 minutes on each side or until cooked through and golden. Repeat with remaining mixture.

Serves 6

Take care when cutting turnips and swedes as they are tough roots. Always use a sharp knife and insert the blade into the heart of the root before you cut it in two, then slice, cube or prepare as desired.

SWEET TURNIP SAUTE

500 g/1 lb turnips, thinly sliced
1 tablespoon sugar
2 tablespoons olive oil
2 teaspoons flour
$^1/_2$ cup/125 mL/4 fl oz chicken stock

1   Place turnips in a bowl, sprinkle with sugar and set aside to stand for 5 minutes. Heat oil in a frying pan over a medium heat, add turnips and cook, stirring, for 4 minutes or until golden brown and cooked through.

2   Place flour in a bowl and gradually whisk in stock until smooth. Pour stock mixture over turnips, bring to the boil and cook for 2 minutes or until sauce thickens. Serve immediately.

Serves 4

Choose firm, young, small to medium-sized turnips which are heavy for their size. Avoid those which are blemished or have moist spots. Tops should be bright and fresh looking.

Salmon on Celeriac Canapés

SALMON ON CELERIAC CANAPES

1 small celeriac, quartered and cut
into 5 mm/^{1}/4 in thick slices
155 g/5 oz sliced smoked salmon
2 tablespoons sour cream
2 tablespoons black caviar
1 bunch/250 g/8 oz fresh watercress,
broken into sprigs

Place celeriac triangles on a serving
platter and top each with a slice of
salmon, then with a little sour cream
and caviar and garnish with watercress.
Cover and refrigerate until required.

Makes 32

Rather ugly in appearance,
once peeled, celeriac
reveals its creamy-white
flesh that has a delightfully
mild celery taste.

57

CELERIAC WITH HOLLANDAISE SAUCE

Microwave

1 large carrot, cut into
5 mm/^{1}/4 in slices
500 g/1 lb celeriac, cut into thin strips
HOLLANDAISE SAUCE
60 g/2 oz butter
^{1}/4 cup/60 mL/2 fl oz cream (double)
2 egg yolks
1 tablespoon lemon juice

1   Using a vegetable cutter, cut a circle from the centre of each carrot slice, forming a ring. Fill carrot rings with bundles of celeriac strips. Place rings in a shallow microwavable dish, cover and cook on HIGH (100%) for 3 minutes.

2   To make sauce, place butter in a microwavable jug and melt on HIGH (100%) for 20-30 seconds. Whisk in cream, egg yolks and lemon juice and cook, stirring every 30 seconds, on MEDIUM (70%) for 1^1/2-2 minutes or until sauce is thick. Drizzle sauce over carrot and celeriac bundles and serve immediately.

Serves 8

Choose small to medium-sized celeriac which are heavy for their size. Select those with the least knobbly surface, as they will peel more easily.

OSSO BUCCO CELERIAC

30 g/1 oz butter
1 clove garlic, crushed
1 onion, chopped
1 kg/2 lb veal shank, cut into pieces
for osso bucco
2 tablespoons flour
2 cups/500 mL/16 fl oz chicken stock
^{1}/2 cup/125 mL/4 fl oz water
^{1}/4 cup/60 mL/2 fl oz port
2 tablespoons tomato paste (purée)
375 g/12 oz celeriac, thinly sliced
125 g/4 oz button mushrooms, sliced

1   Melt butter in a frying pan over a medium heat, add garlic and onion and cook, stirring, for 5 minutes or until onion is tender. Add veal pieces to pan and cook for 4 minutes each side, or until well brown. Using a slotted spoon, remove veal and set aside.

2   Add flour to pan juices and cook, stirring, for 1 minute. Remove pan from heat and gradually whisk in stock, water, port and tomato paste (purée). Return pan to heat and, stirring, bring to the boil. Return veal to pan, reduce heat, cover and simmer for 1 hour or until veal is just tender.

3   Add celeriac and mushrooms to pan and cook for 30 minutes longer or until meat and celeriac are tender.

Serves 4

Wash celeriac well, cut off top and base, peel thinly. To prevent cut surfaces from browning, place in a bowl of water 'acidulated' with a little lemon juice or cider vinegar. The fresher or younger the celeriac, the less likely it is to discolour.

Chicken with Kohlrabi Stuffing

CHICKEN WITH KOHLRABI STUFFING

15 g/¹/₂ oz butter
2 kohlrabi, grated
1 green eating apple, grated
1 tablespoon chopped fresh herbs or
1 teaspoon dried mixed herbs
1 cup/60 g/2 oz breadcrumbs, made
from stale bread
1.5-2 kg/3-4 lb roasting chicken
¹/₄ cup/60 mL/2 fl oz lemon juice
chicken stock

1   Melt butter in a large frying pan over a medium heat, add kohlrabi, apple and herbs and cook, stirring, for 5 minutes or until all liquid evaporates. Remove pan from heat and stir in breadcrumbs.

2   Wash chicken, pat dry with absorbent kitchen paper and fill cavity with kohlrabi mixture. Truss bird, tying legs to tail, and place in a baking dish. Pour lemon juice over chicken and pour stock into the baking dish to a depth of 2 cm/³/₄ in. Bake for 1¹/₂ hours or until chicken is golden brown and cooked through, basting occasionally.

Serves 6

Oven temperature
180°C, 350°F, Gas 4

The name kohlrabi is adapted from the German words 'kohl' meaning cabbage and 'rabi' meaning turnip. Rightly so, as this vegetable looks like a turnip and tastes similar to cabbage.

BEEF AND KOHLRABI CASSEROLE

Oven temperature
180°C, 350°F, Gas 4

Select young, tender kohlrabi bulbs with fresh leaves. Avoid those that are badly scarred or blemished. The smaller the bulb, the more delicate the flavour and texture.

2 kohlrabi, diced
1 kg/2 lb lean stewing steak, cubed
6 pickling onions or mature spring onion bulbs, chopped
250 g/8 oz carrots, chopped
3 stalks celery, chopped
2 bay leaves
$^1/_2$ cup/60 g/2 oz flour
440 g/14 oz canned beef consommé
4 tablespoons tomato paste (purée)
2 tablespoons French mustard

1 Place kohlrabi, steak, onions, carrots, celery and bay leaves in a large casserole dish and toss to combine.

2 Place flour in a bowl and gradually whisk in consommé, tomato paste (purée) and mustard. Add to casserole dish, mix to combine, cover and bake for 2 hours or until beef is tender.

Serves 6

JERUSALEM ARTICHOKE GRATIN

Oven temperature
180°C, 350°F, Gas 4

The Jerusalem artichoke is crisp and sweet. Resembling ginger in appearance, its crunchy flesh tastes similar to water chestnuts and potato.

$^1/_2$ cup/125 mL/4 fl oz cream (double)
$^1/_2$ cup/125 mL/4 fl oz milk
1 tablespoon Dijon mustard
1 kg/1 lb Jerusalem artichokes, peeled and thinly sliced
4 spring onions, chopped
60 g/2 oz grated tasty cheese (mature Cheddar)

1 Place cream, milk and mustard in a bowl and whisk to combine.

2 Line the base of a shallow ovenproof dish with half the artichokes. Sprinkle over half the spring onions and pour over half the cream mixture. Repeat layers, then sprinkle with cheese and bake for 45 minutes or until topping is golden brown. The artichokes will remain crunchy.

Serves 6

Jerusalem Artichoke Salad

1 tablespoon mayonnaise
1 tablespoon French dressing
250 g/8 oz Jerusalem artichokes,
peeled and cut into thin strips
90 g/3 oz prosciutto or ham, cut into
thin strips
1 tablespoon snipped fresh chives
2 ripe avocados, stoned and halved

Place mayonnaise and dressing in a large bowl and mix to combine. Add artichokes, prosciutto or ham and chives and toss to coat. Place avocado halves on four individual serving plates. Top with artichoke salad and serve immediately.

Serves 4

Jerusalem Artichoke Salad

Select firm, medium-sized Jerusalem artichokes, free of mould and soft spots. Store in a plastic food bag in the refrigerator for up to 2 weeks. Scrub well or peel. They may be used raw or cooked. Most recipes for potatoes or celeriac are also suitable for Jerusalem artichokes.

POTATOES

Whatever its name internationally – 'patata' to 'pomme de terre', the potato and its close friend the sweet potato, are the staple of the vegetable world. Like flour or rice, potatoes are at the core of every cook's repertoire. Here are more marvellous ways to serve these favoured tubers, just in case you're looking!

CHEESY POTATO CROQUETTES

750 g/1¹/₂ lb potatoes
100 g/3¹/₂ oz chive-flavoured
cheese spread
15 g/¹/₂ oz butter
1 tablespoon milk
pinch cayenne pepper
¹/₄ cup/30 g/1 oz flour
2 eggs, beaten
¹/₂ cup/30 g/1 oz breadcrumbs, made
from stale bread
vegetable oil for deep-frying

1 Place potatoes in a saucepan, cover with cold water and bring to the boil. Reduce heat and simmer for 20 minutes or until tender. Drain and set aside to cool slightly. Place potatoes, cheese spread, butter, milk and cayenne pepper in a bowl and mash. Cover and refrigerate until cold.

2 Shape potato mixture into 3 cm/ 1¹/₄ in balls and toss in flour, shaking off any excess. Dip in egg and roll in breadcrumbs to coat. Place on a plate lined with plastic food wrap and refrigerate for 15 minutes.

3 Heat oil in a saucepan over a medium heat until a cube of bread browns in 50 seconds. Cook croquettes, a few at a time, for 3-4 minutes or until golden and heated through. Using a slotted spoon, remove croquettes, drain on absorbent kitchen paper and serve immediately.

Makes 16

There are over 400 varieties of potatoes – and names! Its better to understand their uses by their ages instead of names. New potatoes (either red or brown) are newly dug at the beginning of the season. Low in starch with waxy, firm textures and thin skins, new potatoes are used for boiling, roasting, in casseroles and salads. Old potatoes have been left longer in the ground to mature. They are higher in starch and somewhat mealy which makes them more suitable for frying and for jacket-baking.

New Potato and Avocado Salad

New Potato and Avocado Salad

1 kg/2 lb small new potatoes

AVOCADO CREAM DRESSING
1 ripe avocado, stoned, peeled and mashed
1/2 cup/125 g/4 oz sour cream
2 spring onions, thinly sliced
2 tablespoons Italian dressing or lemon juice
1 teaspoon chilli garlic sauce

1 Place potatoes in a saucepan, cover with cold water and bring to the boil. Reduce heat and simmer for 20 minutes or until just tender. Drain and set aside to cool slightly. Place in a salad bowl.

2 To make dressing, place avocado, sour cream, spring onions, dressing or lemon juice and chilli garlic sauce in a bowl and mix to combine. Spoon over potatoes and toss to coat.

Serves 8

Choose smooth, firm potatoes with no wrinkles, cracks, bruises, decay or green areas. A small amount of sprouting does not affect edibility.

CREAMY POTATOES WITH BACON

Microwave

Store potatoes in a cool, dry, well-ventilated area. Keep away from direct light. Remove from plastic bags as soon as possible to prevent greening. Remove any green areas from potatoes before cooking. Peel as thinly as possible to avoid waste and vitamin loss or leave skin intact.

155 g/5 oz bacon, chopped
2 onions, chopped
1 kg/2 lb waxy potatoes, quartered
^{3}/4 cup/185 mL/6 fl oz cream (double)
freshly ground black pepper

Place bacon and onions in a microwavable dish, cover and cook on HIGH (100%) for 5 minutes. Add potatoes, cream and black pepper to taste, cover and cook, stirring occasionally, for 12-15 minutes or until potatoes are just tender. Stand, covered for 5 minutes before serving.

Serves 6

SWEET POTATO CARIBBEAN

500 g/1 lb white sweet potato, diced
1 cup/250 mL/8 fl oz chicken stock
2 firm-ripe bananas, thinly sliced
^{1}/2 cup/125 mL/4 fl oz cream (double)
^{1}/4 cup/60 mL/2 fl oz milk
3 tablespoons snipped fresh chives
1 tablespoon grated fresh Parmesan cheese

1   Place sweet potato in a bowl of cold water and set aside to soak for 30 minutes. Drain potato and place in a saucepan, add stock and bring to the boil over a medium heat. Reduce heat, cover and simmer for 5 minutes. Drain potato. Reserve ^{1}/2 cup/125 mL/4 fl oz stock and return potatoes to saucepan.

2   Add bananas, cream, milk, chives and reserved stock to the sweet potato, cover and cook, stirring occasionally, for 3 minutes. Transfer mixture to an ovenproof dish, sprinkle with Parmesan cheese and cook under a preheated hot grill until top is golden.

Serves 6

The sweet potato is not related to the potato at all, but to the vine morning glory!

SWEET POTATO AND CHICKEN TERRINE

1 kg/2 lb large eggplants (aubergines),
cut lengthwise into 5 cm/2 in slices
salt
500 g/1 lb orange sweet potato, diced
3 eggs
freshly ground black pepper
500 g/1 lb boneless chicken breast
fillets, chopped
1 leek, sliced
1 tablespoon olive oil

1 Rub salt onto eggplant (aubergine) slices, place on absorbent kitchen paper and set aside to stand for 20 minutes.

2 Place potato in a saucepan of boiling water and simmer for 10 minutes or until tender. Drain and set aside to cool slightly. Place potato in a food processor or blender, add 2 eggs and black pepper to taste and process until smooth. Transfer purée to a bowl and set aside.

3 Place chicken, leek and remaining egg in a clean food processor or blender and process until minced. Transfer to a bowl and set aside.

4 Rinse eggplant (aubergine) slices under running water and pat dry on absorbent kitchen paper. Brush both sides of eggplant (aubergine) lightly with oil and cook under a preheated hot grill for 5 minutes each side or until golden.

5 Line the base and sides of an 11 x 21 cm/4^1/$_2$ x 8^1/$_2$ in loaf tin with greaseproof paper and then with overlapping slices of eggplant (aubergine), reserving enough to cover the top. Spoon potato purée into tin, top with chicken mixture and pack down firmly, then top with remaining eggplant (aubergine) slices. Cover with foil and bake for 1 hour or until loaf is firm. Serve hot or cold.

Serves 6

Oven temperature
160°C, 325°F, Gas 3

White sweet potato has pale yellow flesh and a dry mealy texture. Orange sweet potato – also known as yam or kumera – has yellow to deep-orange flesh and a pleasantly sweet chestnut flavour.

VEGETABLE MEDLEY

Globe artichokes, okra, bok choy and witloof chicory are among the many vegetables enjoying a resurgence of interest. Some are old favourites; others, like witloof chicory and alfalfa are 'new' designer leaves and seed sprouts for which experimental cooks love to find new uses.

MUSHROOM AND CHEESE TARTS

Oven temperature
200°C, 400°F, Gas 6

Cultivated mushrooms are sold in three stages of growth. 'Buttons' are small, white and tightly closed with a mild flavour ideal for salads and sauces. 'Cups' have a full-bodied flavour and firm texture and are excellent for pies, casseroles and soups. 'Flats' are fully open and mature with a stronger flavour; use these with meat dishes, fish and bacon.

500 g/1 lb prepared puff pastry
4 large cup mushrooms, stems removed
milk

BACON AND CHEESE FILLING
15 g/^{1}/$_2$ oz butter
2 rashers bacon, chopped
4 spring onions, chopped
1 tablespoon breadcrumbs, made from stale bread
60 g/2 oz creamy blue vein cheese

RICH CHEESE SAUCE
2 teaspoons cornflour
1 cup/250 mL/8 fl oz cream (double)
60g/2 oz creamy blue vein cheese

1   Roll out half the pastry to 3 mm/^{1}/$_8$ in thick, place mushrooms on pastry and cut out two circles for each, 2 cm/^{3}/$_4$ in larger than the mushroom. Reserve pastry scraps.

2   To make filling, melt butter in a frying pan over a medium heat, add bacon and spring onions and cook, stirring, for 3 minutes or until spring onions are soft. Cool slightly, then stir in breadcrumbs and cheese.

3   Divide filling between mushrooms. Place each mushroom on one of its pastry circles. Brush edges with a little water, top with second pastry circle and crimp edges to seal. Decorate tarts with pastry scraps and place on baking trays. Brush with milk and bake for 20 minutes or until pastry is puffed and golden.

4   To make sauce, place cornflour in a small saucepan and whisk in cream. Add cheese and cook over a low heat, stirring constantly, for 5 minutes or until cheese melts and sauce thickens. Serve sauce with tarts.

Serves 4

Mushroom and Cheese Tarts

Mushroom and Ham Rice

Avoid mushrooms that are dry, wrinkled or slimy in appearance. Store mushrooms in a cloth or paper bag in the refrigerator. Never store in plastic. Wipe with a damp cloth, or clean lightly with a pastry brush. Stems may be removed or left intact depending on use.

60 g/2 oz butter
375 g/12 oz button mushrooms, sliced
125 g/4 oz ham, diced
1^1/2 cups/330 g/10^1/2 oz white rice
2 cups/500 mL/16 fl oz chicken stock
^{1}/2 cup/125 mL/4 fl oz white wine
1 tablespoon chopped fresh oregano or
1 teaspoon dried oregano
freshly ground black pepper

1   Melt butter in a frying pan over a medium heat, add mushrooms and ham and cook, stirring, for 3-4 minutes or until mushrooms are just cooked.

2   Add rice, stock, wine, oregano and black pepper to taste to pan and bring to the boil. Reduce heat, cover and simmer for 20 minutes or until all liquid is absorbed and rice is tender.

Serves 6

Chicken and Mushroom Soup

15 g/^{1}/2 oz butter
500 g/1 lb flat mushrooms, thinly sliced
1 onion, chopped
^{1}/4 cup/60 mL/2 fl oz dry sherry
250 g/8 oz boneless chicken breast fillets, thinly sliced
4 cups/1 litre/1^3/4 pt chicken stock
^{1}/4 cup/60 mL/2 fl oz soy sauce
1 tablespoon sugar
155 g/5 oz tofu, cut into 1 cm/^{1}/2 in cubes
2 spring onions, finely chopped

Rich in B-group vitamins, mushrooms are a good source of dietary fibre and protein. For a vegetarian main course soup, omit the chicken and increase the tofu to 250g/8 oz.

1   Melt butter in a large saucepan over a medium heat, add mushrooms and onion and cook, stirring, for 2-3 minutes or until onion is golden. Add sherry to pan and simmer for 1 minute.

2   Stir in chicken, stock, soy sauce and sugar and bring to the boil. Reduce heat, cover and simmer for 7 minutes or until chicken is cooked. Add tofu and spring onions and heat for 3-4 minutes or until heated through. Serve immediately.

Serves 4

Globe Artichoke and Tuna Salad

GLOBE ARTICHOKE AND TUNA SALAD

6 globe artichokes, trimmed
$^1/4$ cup/60 mL/2 fl oz lemon juice
220 g/7 oz canned tuna, drained and
flaked
45 g/1$^1/2$ oz pitted black olives, sliced
2 spring onions, chopped
200 g/6$^1/2$ oz natural yogurt
2 tablespoons mayonnaise
freshly ground black pepper

1   Bring a saucepan of water to the boil, add artichokes and lemon juice. Reduce heat and simmer for 20-25 minutes or until stems are tender when pierced. Drain and plunge artichokes into iced water to cool. Pull out all outer leaves from artichokes until the compact heart is revealed. Reserve leaves. Trim the base from each heart, remove and discard the hairy choke.

2   Chop artichoke hearts and place in a bowl, add tuna, olives, spring onions, yogurt and mayonnaise and mix to combine. Season to taste with black pepper. Spoon mixture into the centre of six individual plates and arrange artichoke leaves around the edge. Serve cold.

Serves 6

To prepare artichokes for cooking: use a stainless steel knife to slice off stem. Remove and discard coarse outer leaves, then cut one-third off from the top of the artichoke. Snip off any remaining thorny tips with scissors. Rinse well.

Artichokes with Wine Butter

$^1/_2$ cup/125 mL/4 fl oz lemon juice
water
4 globe artichokes, trimmed
$1^1/_2$ cups/375 mL/12 fl oz white wine
90 g/3 oz butter, chopped

Hollandaise sauce or a homemade mayonnaise flavoured with Dijon mustard and anchovy paste are two more delicious companions for artichokes. To eat an artichoke with a dipping sauce, simply pull out leaves, one at a time, from the artichoke, dip into the sauce and scrape the edible flesh from the leaf with your teeth. The remaining coarse leaf is then discarded.

1   Place lemon juice and 3 cm/1$^1/_4$ in water in a large saucepan, place artichokes upright in pan and bring to the boil over a medium heat. Reduce heat, cover and simmer for 20-25 minutes or until stems are tender when pierced.

2   Place wine in a small saucepan and bring to the boil over a medium heat. Reduce heat and simmer for 10-15 minutes or until liquid is reduced to $^1/_2$ cup/125 mL/4 fl oz. Whisk butter into wine, a piece at a time, until butter melts, ingredients are combined and sauce is glossy. Serve sauce immediately with artichokes.

Serves 4

Artichokes with Tomato Sauce

4 globe artichokes
$^1/_4$ cup/60 mL/2 fl oz vinegar

TOMATO HAM SAUCE
15 g/$^1/_2$ oz butter
100 g/3$^1/_2$ oz ham, chopped
2 spring onions, chopped
$1^1/_2$ cups/375 mL/12 fl oz dry
white wine
1 tablespoon chopped fresh basil or
1 teaspoon dried basil
1 tablespoon tomato paste (purée)

Choose tight, compact, fresh, bright green artichokes with plump heads that feel heavy for their size (overall size has no bearing on flavour). Browning may mean old age or bruising. The edible portions are the lower fleshy parts of the leaves.

1   To make sauce, melt butter in a saucepan over a medium heat, add ham, spring onions, wine, basil and tomato paste (purée) and bring to the boil. Reduce heat and simmer until sauce is reduced by half. Set aside and keep warm.

2   Bring a large saucepan of water to the boil, add artichokes and vinegar and simmer for 20-25 minutes or until stems are tender when pierced. Drain artichokes, cut in half and remove hairy chokes. Arrange artichoke halves on individual plates, drizzle with sauce and serve immediately.

Serves 4

Watercress Dressing served with grilled fish cutlets

WATERCRESS DRESSING

4 boneless chicken breast fillets or
4 fish cutlets

WATERCRESS DRESSING
$^1/_2$ bunch/300 g/9$^1/_2$ oz watercress
2 cloves garlic
$^1/_2$ cup/125 mL/4 fl oz herb-flavoured
vinegar
1 tablespoon honey
1 teaspoon Dijon mustard
$^1/_2$ cup/125 mL/4 fl oz walnut or
vegetable oil

1 Cook chicken or fish under a
preheated medium grill or on a barbecue
for 5 minutes each side or until cooked.

2 To make dressing, place watercress
in a food processor or blender and
process until chopped. Add garlic,
vinegar, honey and mustard and process
until combined. With machine
running, gradually add oil and process
until smooth. Serve with chicken or
fish – also delicious as a sauce for pasta
or a dressing for salads.

Serves 4

Watercress has a spicy,
peppery flavour, and is
used mainly for garnishes,
but makes delicious soups,
sauces, salads and
mousses.

71

FRENCH-STYLE WATERCRESS SOUP

15 g/¹/₂ oz butter
2 onions, finely chopped
1 tablespoon flour
3¹/₂ cups/875 mL/1¹/₂ pt chicken
stock
100 g/3¹/₂ oz watercress, chopped
freshly ground black pepper

1   Melt butter in a saucepan over a medium heat, add onions and cook, stirring, for 3-4 minutes or until onions are golden. Add flour to pan and cook, stirring, for 1 minute. Remove pan from heat and gradually stir in stock. Return pan to heat and bring to the boil. Reduce heat and simmer, stirring occasionally, for 10 minutes.

2   Stir in watercress and black pepper to taste and serve immediately.

Serves 4

Watercress should have dark green, fresh-looking leaves that are crisp, tender and free of dirt or yellow leaves.

SESAME WATERCRESS STIR-FRY

1 tablespoon olive oil
1 teaspoon sesame oil
100 g/3¹/₂ oz fresh shiitake
mushrooms, sliced
1 red pepper, sliced
1 bunch/250 g/8 oz watercress,
broken into sprigs
2 tablespoons teriyaki sauce
1 tablespoon sesame seeds, toasted

Heat olive and sesame oils in a wok or frying pan over a medium heat, add mushrooms and red pepper and stir-fry for 2-3 minutes or until mushrooms are just tender. Add watercress and teriyaki sauce and stir-fry for 2-3 minutes or until watercress is just cooked. Sprinkle with sesame seeds and serve immediately.

Serves 4

To store fresh watercress, place it in a bowl containing a small amount of water. Cover with plastic food wrap and refrigerate up to 1 week.

Chicory and Camembert Salad

CHICORY AND CAMEMBERT SALAD

1-2 witloof chicory, separated
assorted lettuce leaves
2 oranges, segmented
125 g/4 oz Camembert cheese, cut
into thin wedges
mustard cress or watercress

CURRANT JELLY DRESSING
¹/₄ cup/90 g/3 oz redcurrant jelly
¹/₃ cup/90 mL/3 fl oz olive oil
¹/₄ cup/60 mL/2 fl oz red wine vinegar
freshly ground black pepper

1   Arrange chicory and lettuce leaves in a large salad bowl, add oranges, Camembert cheese and mustard cress or watercress and toss to combine.

2   To make dressing, melt redcurrant jelly in a small saucepan over a medium heat. Place melted jelly, oil, vinegar and black pepper to taste in a screwtop jar, shake well to combine and drizzle over salad. Serve immediately.

Serves 6

Also known as Belgian endive and French endive, witloof chicory has small tender heads of white leaves that have a slightly bitter flavour.

CHICORY WITH BRANDY MUSTARD

45 g/1 1/2 oz butter
6 witloof chicory, quartered
1/4 cup/60 mL/2 fl oz brandy
2 teaspoons wholegrain mustard
freshly ground black pepper

1 Melt butter in a frying pan over a medium heat, add chicory and cook, turning occasionally, for 2 minutes or until just wilted. Remove chicory and arrange on serving plates.

2 Stir brandy into pan, heat until fumes appear, then ignite brandy with a lighted taper. Stir in mustard and black pepper to taste. Drizzle sauce over chicory and serve immediately.

Serves 6

Select crisp, compact, small heads of witloof chicory. Leaves should be bright white and have a pale yellow to green, tender frill. Avoid those with brown discolouration or loosely packed leaves.

OVEN BRAISED CHICORY

6 witloof chicory, cut in half lengthwise
1/4 cup/60 mL/ 2 fl oz lemon juice
45 g/1 1/2 oz butter, chopped
1/4 cup chopped fresh basil or
2 teaspoons dried basil
1 teaspoon sugar
1 cup/250 mL/8 fl oz chicken stock

Place chicory in a small baking dish, top with lemon juice, butter pieces, basil and sugar. Pour over stock, cover with a lid or foil and bake for 25-30 minutes, turning once, or until chicory is tender. Serve hot.

Serves 6

Oven temperature
180°C, 350°F, Gas4

This recipe is also a good way of cooking celery, leeks and any variety of cabbage.

Deep-fried Okra

DEEP-FRIED OKRA

500 g/1 lb okra
1 egg
2 teaspoons Worcestershire sauce
1 clove garlic, crushed
Tabasco sauce
vegetable oil for deep-frying
1 cup/125 g/4 oz flour

1   Bring a saucepan of water to the boil over a medium heat, add okra and simmer for 5 minutes. Drain and set aside to cool. Place egg, Worcestershire sauce, garlic and Tabasco sauce to taste in a bowl and whisk to combine.

2   Heat vegetable oil in a large saucepan until a cube of bread dropped in browns in 50 seconds. Dip okra into egg mixture then toss in flour to coat, shaking off any excess. Add okra a few pieces at a time and cook for 3-4 minutes or until golden. Using a slotted spoon, remove okra and drain on absorbent kitchen paper. Serve immediately.

Serves 10

More commonly disguised in braises and casseroles, the true flavour and texture of okra take centre stage in this light tempura-style party dish. Serve with a favourite dipping sauce as an hors-d'oeuvres or accompaniment to meat, chicken or fish.

OKRA AND CRABMEAT GUMBO

45 g/1^1/$_2$ oz butter
2 onions, chopped
1 red pepper, chopped
1 clove garlic, crushed
6 cups/1.5 litres/2^1/$_2$ pt chicken stock
250 g/8 oz tomatoes, chopped
300 g/9^1/$_2$ oz okra, thinly sliced
Tabasco sauce
^{1}/$_4$ cup/60 g/2 oz white rice
200 g/6^1/$_2$ oz canned crab meat,
drained
freshly ground black pepper

1   Melt butter in a saucepan over a medium heat, add onions, red pepper and garlic and cook, stirring, for 2-3 minutes or until onions are golden. Stir in stock, tomatoes, okra, and Tabasco sauce to taste and bring to the boil. Reduce heat and simmer, uncovered, for 10 minutes.

2   Stir in rice, cover and simmer for 20 minutes or until rice is tender. Add crab meat and black pepper to taste and cook, stirring gently, for 3-4 minutes or until heated through. Serve immediately.

Serves 6-8

Added to soups and casseroles, okra's sticky composition has the ability to thicken.

OKRA VEGETABLE CURRY

2 tablespoons olive oil
1 teaspoon curry powder
^{1}/$_4$ teaspoon ground cumin
500 g/1 lb okra, cut into
2 cm/^{3}/$_4$ in slices
500 g/1 lb potatoes, diced
2 onions, sliced
1 red pepper, chopped
1 fresh red chilli, chopped
1 cup/250 mL/8 fl oz chicken stock

1   Heat oil in a large frying pan over a medium heat, add curry powder and cumin and cook, stirring, for 1 minute or until fragrant. Add okra, potatoes, onions, red pepper and chilli to pan and cook, stirring, for 2-3 minutes or until onions are golden.

2   Stir stock into pan and bring to the boil. Reduce heat, cover and simmer for 15 minutes or until potatoes are just tender.

Serves 6

Select small to medium pods of okra that are firm, crisp and bright in colour. Pods should snap easily when broken. Store in a plastic food bag in the refrigerator. Okra is best used within 2-3 days of purchasing.

Herbed Garlic Squash

HERBED GARLIC SQUASH

250 g/8 oz yellow patty pan squash,
sliced
250 g/8 oz green patty pan squash,
sliced
60 g/2 oz butter
3 cloves garlic, crushed
2 tablespoons chopped fresh herbs

1 Boil, steam or microwave squash
until just tender. Drain, place in a
serving dish, set aside and keep warm.

2 Melt butter in a frying pan over a
medium heat, add garlic and herbs and
cook, stirring, for 2-3 minutes or until
garlic is golden. Drizzle butter mixture
over squash and serve immediately.

Serves 6

When squash are
unavailable, green or
yellow zucchini (courgettes)
can be used instead.

QUICK SQUASH PROVENÇAL

Select firm, medium-sized squash, heavy for their size. Look for smooth, glossy skin, free of soft spots.

500 g/1 lb patty pan squash, halved or zucchini (courgettes), sliced
1 green pepper, cut into julienne strips
1 cup/250 mL/8 fl oz prepared tomato pasta sauce
1 tablespoon chopped fresh basil or 1 teaspoon dried basil
freshly ground black pepper

Place squash or zucchini (courgettes), green pepper, pasta sauce, basil and black pepper to taste in a saucepan and bring to the boil over a medium heat. Reduce heat, cover and simmer for 10-15 minutes or until squash or zucchini (courgettes) are tender.

Serves 6

SQUASH WITH ONIONS

A little diced bacon cooked with the onion, will make a satisfying addition to this recipe.

15 g/^{1}/2 oz butter
1 red onion, finely chopped
500 g/1 lb patty pan squash or zucchini (courgettes), thinly sliced
2 teaspoons Worcestershire sauce

Melt butter in a frying pan over a medium heat, add onion and cook, stirring, for 2 minutes or until onion is tender. Add squash or zucchini (courgettes) and Worcestershire sauce to pan, mix to combine, cover and cook for 5-10 minutes or until squash or zucchini (courgettes) are tender.

Serves 6

Alfalfa Fishburgers

ALFALFA FISHBURGERS

Microwave

500 g/1 lb boneless white fish fillets,
sliced
3 tablespoons snipped fresh dill
75 g/2¹/₂ oz alfalfa sprouts
freshly ground black pepper
chilli sauce
4 hamburger buns
1 tomato, sliced
4 tablespoons mayonnaise

1   Place fish, dill, about 3 tablespoons alfalfa sprouts, black pepper and chilli sauce to taste in a food processor or blender and process until smooth. Shape mixture into four patties.

2   Place patties in a shallow microwavable dish, cover and cook on MEDIUM-HIGH (70%) for 5 minutes or until cooked. Alternatively, pan-fry patties in a little butter and oil for 2-3 minutes on each side or until cooked.

3   Split buns in half and place remaining sprouts on the bases. Top with slices of tomato, then patties. Spoon mayonnaise over patties and top with bun tops. Serve immediately.

Serves 4

Alfalfa sprouts are germinated seeds, technically a form of lucerne or cattle feed, prized for their succulent soft-green baby shoots and white roots.

ALFALFA AND CHICKEN SALAD

1 cup/250 mL/8 fl oz white wine
1 cup/250 mL/8 fl oz water
4 boneless chicken breast fillets
45 g/1^1/$_2$ oz alfalfa sprouts
1 red pepper, chopped
1 green pepper, chopped
6 spring onions, chopped
^{1}/$_2$ cup/125 mL/4 fl oz mayonnaise
2 tablespoons raspberry or cider vinegar

1 Place wine and water in a frying pan and bring to the boil over a medium heat. Add chicken and poach for 4 minutes or until just tender. Set aside to cool in the liquid, then drain.

2 To serve, arrange alfalfa, red and green pepper and spring onions on a serving platter. Top with chicken breasts. Combine mayonnaise and vinegar and spoon over chicken.

Serves 4

FRIED ALFALFA BALLS

6 slices bread
1 onion, roughly chopped
6 tablespoons chopped fresh coriander, mint or parsley
freshly ground black pepper
45 g/1^1/$_2$ oz alfalfa sprouts
vegetable oil for shallow frying

1 Place bread, onion, herbs and black pepper to taste in a food processor or blender and process until smooth. Transfer mixture to a bowl, add alfalfa sprouts and mix to combine.

2 Shape mixture into walnut-sized balls. Heat vegetable oil in a large frying pan until a cube of bread browns in 50 seconds and cook balls, a few at a time, for 3-4 minutes or until golden. Using a slotted spoon, remove balls and drain on absorbent kitchen paper. Serve immediately.

Makes 15

Bok Choy Parcel

BOK CHOY PARCEL

250 g/8 oz prepared puff pastry
milk
1 tablespoon poppy seeds

BOK CHOY AND RICE FILLING
15 g/^{1}/$_2$ oz butter
1 onion, finely chopped
1 carrot, finely chopped
1 red pepper, cut into thin strips
1 bunch bok choy, thinly sliced
^{1}/$_2$ cup/100 g/3^1/$_2$ oz white rice,
cooked
1 egg, beaten
1 tablespoon grated Parmesan cheese

1   To make filling, melt butter in a large frying pan over a medium heat, add onion, carrot and red pepper and cook, stirring, for 5 minutes or until vegetables are golden. Add bok choy and cook, stirring, for 3 minutes or until vegetables are just tender. Stir rice into vegetable mixture, remove pan from heat and set aside to cool. Stir egg and Parmesan cheese into cooled mixture.

2   Roll pastry out to make a 40 x 25 cm/ 16 x 10 in rectangle. Spoon filling down the length of the pastry and roll up, tucking ends in, to form a parcel. Place on a greased baking tray, brush lightly with milk and sprinkle with poppy seeds. Bake for 30-35 minutes or until pastry is crisp and golden.

Serves 8

Oven temperature
200°C, 400°F, Gas 6

Bok Choy is also known as Chinese chard, Chinese white cabbage, buck choy and pak choy. There are numerous different types of bok choy, each with its different Asian name.

INDEX

INDEX